THROUGH THE EYES
OF THE EAGLE

H. Wolofsky, founder of the *Keneder Odler*.
From *The Jew in Canada*, 1926.

Through the Eyes of The Eagle

THE EARLY MONTREAL YIDDISH PRESS
(1907-1916)

TRANSLATED FROM THE YIDDISH BY

David Rome

EDITED AND INTRODUCED BY
PIERRE ANCTIL

Véhicule Press

Published with the assistance of The Canada Council for the Arts, the Book Publishing Industry Development Program of the Department of Canadian Heritage, and the Société de développement des entreprise culturelles du Québec (SODEC).

The publisher would like to thank Janice Rosen of the Canadian Jewish Congress National Archives, the Canadian Jewish Congress National Archives Committee, the Institut québécois de recherche sur la culture juive (IQECJ), and Jack Wolofsky for their support.

Cover design: J.W. Stewart
Editorial consultant: Janice Rosen
Translations from the French of the introductory essays
were done by Janice Rosen, beginning on pages 9, 15, 31, 45;
and Phyllis Aronoff, beginning on pages 61, 73, 85, 101, 109, 121,
131, 141, 157, 175
Set in Adobe Minion by Simon Garamond
Printed by AGMV-Marquis Inc.

CATALOGUING IN PUBLICATION DATA
Main entry under title:
Through the eyes of The Eagle : the early Montreal Yiddish press
(1907-1916)

(Dossier Québec series)
Translated from the Yiddish.
ISBN 1-55065-148-x

1. Jews–Quebec (Province)–Montréal–History
–20th century–Sources. 2. Yiddish newspapers–Quebec (Province)
–Montréal–History–20th century. i. Rome, David,
1910-1996. ii. Anctil, Pierre, 1952-   iii. Series

PN5650.T48 2001   971.4'28004924   C2001-901037-0

Published by Véhicule Press
www.vehiculepress.com

Distributed by GDS.

Printed in Canada on alkaline paper.

Contents

David Rome and Jacques Langlais at the launching
of their book on Jews and French Quebecers, 1986.
Photo by Alan Kaufman.
Canadian Jewish Congress National Archives.

David Rome at the Canadian Jewish Congress Archives reading
a page of Purim jokes from the *Keneder Odler* microfilm, c. 1987.
Photo by Henry Granek.
Canadian Jewish Congress National Archives.

Introduction

In 1987 David Rome and Jacques Langlais founded the *Institut québécois d'études sur la culture juive* (IQECJ), a non-profit organization whose principal goal was to make better known, mostly among French-speaking people, the historical and cultural heritage of Montreal's Jewish community. It also endeavoured to make available the documentary sources pertaining to Montreal and Quebec Jewish history, and to ensure the transmission of Montreal Yiddish language and literature.

In 1992 the IQECJ received a significant subsidy from the Minister of Multiculturalism and Citizenship Canada to carry out the translation from Yiddish into English, excerpts drawn from the *Keneder Odler* (The Canadian Eagle) and other Yiddish newspapers in Montreal published just before and during the World War I, as the largest wave of Eastern European Jewish migrants was arriving in the city. The founders of the IQECJ chose this period of Montreal Yiddish literary history because it was relatively unexplored by researchers and because it revealed the goals and experiences of the early immigrants. Most of these immigrants established themselves during the years immediately following the beginnings of the mass Yiddish-speaking immigration to Montreal, 1905 to 1914 — from the Russian insurrection against the Czar to the beginning of the World War I. Their first years in Montreal embodied the circumstances and the debates which were to give rise to the Jewish community in the city. In the space of ten years the new arrivals would set up the nucleus of a Montreal organizational structure which was as much secular as it was religious. They would found ideological movements, establish networks for mutual aid, and launch powerful unions in the St. Lawrence Boulevard area, all using Yiddish, the Jewish lingua franca of Eastern Europe.

During the last years of his life, David Rome translated close to four hundred excerpts from the Yiddish press within the framework of this project. They begin with the editorial from the first issue of the *Keneder Odler* of August 30, 1907 and end with a text published in the *Veg* in February 1916, a period of less than ten years which constitute a turning point in Montreal Jewish history. At the time of the translator's death in 1996 these texts remained in random order and it was not possible to determine how David Rome had intended to classify and present the excerpts in question. In addition, the complete collection of Yiddish press articles and editorials translated by Rome was of uneven quality, and several texts remained unfinished. Obviously, the translator had still been engaged in his work when he was taken from this world. It was deemed not possible, for these reasons, to publish the entirety of the work Rome carried out. Moreover, in a practice well known to the people who worked over a long time with David Rome, he did not always manage to find the exact date of the texts which he had translated, nor their source. The working methods of this historian and archivist little resembles those presently accepted in the academic world. He remained faithful, instead, to those of an ancient Jewish literary continuity of pre-scientific origins, with roots in the grand tradition of Talmudic compilation. Throughout his life David Rome preferred to accumulate information on the many varied topics which interested him, even if partial and incomplete, leaving to others the task of imposing order and finding an end point. It is in this context that his collection of translations from the pre-war period was presented to us. Confronted with this situation, David Rome's successors and fellow members of the IQECJ chose to honour the archivist by respecting his mode of thought, in not modifying the spirit and the letter of his contributions to the field of Yiddish translation.

From the approximately four hundred existing texts, I chose to retain eighty-six for publication. These selections were made in consultation with my IQECJ colleagues, including Janice Rosen of the Canadian Jewish Congress Archives, who worked alongside David Rome from 1986 onward. These excerpts from the Yiddish press were selected according to three criteria: their historical significance and the light they shed on the period of the mass Yiddish-speaking immigration to Montreal; their literary quality; and finally their validity in the field of translation and with regard to their source. In order to verify the information which had been left to us, the organizers of the IQECJ engaged Yiddish scholar Rebecca Margolis, then a McGill University undergraduate student in Jewish Studies, to reread the body of David Rome's translations to check its coherence and to attempt to track down the texts which appeared most problematic. This being said, one can easily surmise that the non-dated and unidentified excerpts included belong in a general sense to the same literary and historical context as rest of the corpus for which David Rome had defined the boundaries. For this reason they are also worthy of the reader's attention.

In the matter of spelling conventions, the standardized YIVO spelling conventions are used, for example, in using "*kh*" to represent the guttural sound traditionally rendered in English transliterations as "*ch.*" The ellipsis (...) is used to indicate places where the translator has omitted a portion of the original text. Square brackets [...] indicate that the text has been para-phrased by the translator. Finally, square brackets are also used to indicate where the original titles of articles could not be confirmed.

In addition to recognizing the many-faceted IQECJ contributions, I wish to gratefully acknowledge the painstaking initial typing and formatting of this work by Phyllis Kimia, formerly of the CJC Archives; and the later revisions ably executed by Hélène Vallée from the Archives; and Bella Lehrer, formerly of CJC, Quebec Region. Janice Rosen, Archives Director, was on hand to supervise and offer assistance at all stages of the project. I also wish to acknowledge the help of Jacques Langlais, Alexis Nouss, and Jack Wolofsky.

Even if it is not strictly speaking signed by David Rome, this work must nonetheless be regarded as the last project conceived and executed by the historian during his long career. My hope, and that of our colleagues, is that our efforts will serve to bridge the often considerable distance which separated these texts from their potential readership, in particular researchers interested in the literary and cultural history of Yiddish Montreal during this crucial period at the beginning of the twentieth century. The work and personality of David Rome has had a major and enduring influence on most of the present organizers of the IQECJ. It is therefore only fair that we now offer him this work in homage.

Pierre Anctil

August 2001

The Montreal
Jewish Context

```
DOMINION OF CANADA
PROVINCE OF QUEBEC
CITY OF MONTREAL
```

A F F I D A V I T

```
          I,SOLOMON ABEL,TAILOR,RESIDING AT
No.3164 St.DOMINIQUE Street,MONTREAL,P.Q.,BEING
DULY SWORN,DO SOLEMNLY DECLARE AND DEPOSE THAT:-

1.        THAT I AM 40 YEARS OF AGE.

2.        THAT I AM NO IDLER;AND AM OCCUPIED IN A
USEFUL OCCUPATION IN THE CITY OF MONTREAL.

3.        THAT I AM MARRIED TO DAME SOFIE SUSKIN
SINCE THE YEAR 1900;AND THAT THE SAID MARRIAGE TOOK
PLACE IN RUSSIA IN ACCORDANCE WITH THE RULES OF THE
HEBREW RELIGION.

4.        THAT I AM THE SOLE SUPPORTER OF MY FAMILY
CONSISTING OF WIFE AND 6 MINOR CHILDREN.

5.        THAT I CAME TO CANADA IN THE YEAR 1907.

6.        THAT I AM A CITIZEN OF CANADA.(NATURALIZED)

7.        THAT I HAVE HEREUNTO ATTACHED MY PHOTOGRAPH
WHICH IS A GOOD AND TRUE LIKENESS OF MYSELF.
```

Witness
S. Thomas
1599 St. Dominique St.

Witness
M. Eibel
17 Malisses St.

```
          AND THAT I MADE THE FOREGOING DECLARATIONS
BELIEVING THEM TO BE TRUE AND CORRECT,AND KNOWING
THAT IT IS OF THE SAME FORCE AND EFFECT AS IF MADE
UNDER OATH AND BY VIRTUE OF THE"CANADA EVIDENCE ACT
 ."OF THE YEAR 1893. AND I SIGNED. Solomon Abel

   SWORN,THIS MAY 21,1918.
Jos. Miller

   A JUSTICE OF THE PEACE
AND A SUPERIOR COURT COMMISSIONER
FOR THE DISTRICT OF THE CITY OF THE MONTREAL.
```

An affidavit sworn by tailor Solomon Abel, attesting
to his good character, May 21, 1918.
Canadian Jewish Congress National Archives

THE YIDDISH LANGUAGE PRESS appeared in Montreal at a time when the Jewish community of the city was at the very beginning of a long process of internal structuring and consolidation. In this environment the Yiddish newspapers, led by the *Keneder Odler*, from the outset assumed the task of facilitating the birth and growth of an entire set of new Yiddish-speaking institutions. They would contribute towards the harmonious adaptation of a wave of Jewish immigration whose size was without precedent in Canadian history. In this sense, they would be an experiment and an innovation of the first order, in the same manner as many of the Jewish organizations which emerged for the first time in the same period. Moreover, as observers who wrote in the Montreal Yiddish newspapers, recent immigrants themselves, noted, this country into which the Eastern European Jews were integrating was itself in the process of emerging and discovering its identity, even as the new inhabitants were arriving en masse upon its shores.

What was Canada at the very beginning of the twentieth century and what characterized its identity? What did it have to offer to Yiddish speakers? How was it distinguishable from its powerful neighbour to the south? These are questions no one could answer with certainty, given the newness of the country, almost as new, in fact, as the Jewish community beginning little by little to settle there. This was the striking reality quickly noted by visitors like Abraham Coralnik, at the time a young journalist from New York, staying for a short while in Montreal. Such conditions were not that unusual at the time within the Jewish diaspora. Already in 1915, Coralnik wrote, one could sense that the Canadian — and the Canadian Jewish — historical framework would prove different from that of the United States.

And in what way? While the great American Jewish communities were undergoing enormous assimilationist pressure, their members trying to conform as quickly as possible to prevailing social and economic canons, in Montreal Yiddish-speaking Jews acted, thought, and spoke with the same accent as their co-religionists in Russia. All things considered, the life of the *shtetl* and the continuation of certain Eastern European traditions seemed completely possible in Canada, while in the United States they confronted insurmountable obstacles. Moreover, Canadians themselves then seemed so uncertain of who they were and how they differed from other peoples that the immigrants in their midst passed relatively unperceived, thereby profiting from a larger margin for maneuverability than elsewhere in North America.

Could it be, wondered Coralnik, that Yiddish speakers discovered in Montreal and in Canada a medium more favourable to the flourishing of their culture?

At the time that these texts appeared, Canadian Jewry was almost entirely commensurate with Montreal Jewry. The observations in Montreal's Yiddish press applied across the country, and already one could sense that the rhythm of development of the community established around St. Lawrence Boulevard would have a decisive influence on the entire Canadian Jewish twentieth century. It is enough to read the description that Rabbi Hirsch Cohen wrote in 1913 of the emerging Jewish institutions in the city to be convinced that the future of Judaism in Canada was to be played out in Montreal, and that no major obstacle lay before it when he wrote. Already by this date the diversity and complexity of the Jewish organizations appeared remarkable in the city and the optimism of its principal organizers was contagious. At this time Eastern European immigrants were still arriving in this city founded by de Maisonneuve, a city where their predecessors of only a few years earlier had already found the means to receive them by establishing the first embryos of a community structure.

Another subject under discussion at that time was the uniqueness of the Jewish immigrants' situation when compared to the rest of the newcomers who were then entering Canada. From 1905 to 1914, until the beginning of the World War I, is the period during which the country admitted the greatest number of new citizens. The Jews, points out journalist and poet Joseph Goodman, did not leave Russia for economic reasons alone, but above all because they were threatened by bloody pogroms and violent methods of political repression. In 1912 Goodman believed that this situation could only continue and that the Canadian Jewish community had to develop the means to receive the new groups of refugees who would certainly come as a result of the conditions of the post-war period. Here was one of the principal motivations which pushed Canadian Jews to establish institutions for the long-term, and to develop an effective and durable community structure.

No overview of the period would be complete without a comment on the breadth of the gap which separated the Montreal Yiddish-speaking immigrants and members of the first Jewish community established in the city during the nineteenth century, whose lifestyle mirrored those citizens of British origin in the general population. The cultural and ideological rupture between *uptowners* and *downtowners* is perfectly summarized in the lampoon delivered by Rabbi Simon Glazer in 1915, which complained about the lack of respect shown by the more established and anglicized Jews towards the aspirations of their newly-arrived Yiddish-speaking co-religionists. The outraged tone, the barely veiled threats, and the feelings of rejection which filter through Glazer's text would define the relationship between these two Montreal sub-communities during the first half of the twentieth century, and prevent the Jews of the city from presenting a united front on certain fundamental issues of interest to both groups.

Circumcision certificate, 1921.
Canadian Jewish Congress National Archives.

The Fourth America
Dr. Abraham Coralnick
Der Veg, December 8, 1915

I have not seen much of this infinitely distant land, barely one city — the biggest city of the country, Montreal, the centre of Canadian cultural life. (...) But from this one city we can see the nature of the land. As you enter it, you wonder, is this America? Can we relate the image we all have of America and of American life — especially of the "first" true real America of today — with the calm, quiet, dare I say, small town Montreal? Quiet streets, old buildings, the calm walk of the people, slow, unhurried: no one rushes, there are many pounds of time; the talk is quiet, sober, restrained.

The thinking is apparently also not so hurried. Life is like that here: small-townish — but only from the perspective of a New Yorker: A European would say it is like Europe.

What is it that is most interesting in Europe? It is not only its age, but the naturalness of everybody there. When we enter a European city, our first impression is that it cannot be otherwise, there are no difficult questions to be asked, there is nothing to be asked just as no one wonders about a forest, about a garden, or a man. He is born so, brought up so, the fruit of generations and an heir of an old heritage. That is the stamp of European culture.

And it seems to me, it is also the stamp of the Canadian. This is the profound difference between Canada and America.

I know that what we call Canada today, what has been so constructed in the endless, distant land, is only a drop in the sea, a tiny portion of a near-continent; that Montreal and the other cities of settlement are but a narrow corridor to the house not yet built.

But the corridor is already not American, not New Yorkish. It is already a little palace with marble walls, stained-glass windows; a corridor already in itself a comfortable home.

We stop at only one side of Montreal, at its Jewish quarter.

As you enter New York or Chicago you first note the Jewish area, the "East Side" in different forms, the "ghetto." There is a sharp line drawn between this East Side and the rest of the world: a wall not to be jumped unless you shed all to which you are accustomed, all that you have inherited. The East Side is a corridor to a corridor, the first, filthiest step to the great depth.

The European man, especially the European Jew, feels lonely and lost as on a distant alien island. He senses that all that had been for him sacred and great, which had sustained and warmed him, is only an unnecessary burden in America; that one needs to change from head to foot.

As I paced the streets of Montreal I wondered: Where am I? In distant Canada or in Old Europe, in some Russian city, in Vitebsk or in Mohilev? Forget the English words on the store signs or the sounds of French and English, and you are under the illusion that you are in the old home. In New York not even an illusion is possible.

It is snowing, the streets become white, velvety. One does not hear people's footsteps. It is silent. The small quiet houses stand as in a dream. About you, you hear Yiddish words, the sounds of the Yiddish language, sounds of home. And the language is not American, not the rapid impudent, loud, resounding Yankee Yiddish, but our own from home. People look at you quietly and comfortably, not with that weary, hungry, curious American glance. It seems I have not travelled far — only from one *guberniye* to another, from the old unfree Russia to a new liberated, more beautiful one. And it seems to me that all who are here, all the Jews who walk these quiet streets, feel and think as I do.

I realize that this is only a very general impression; that when you examine life here more closely, more deeply, it is not so idyllic; that here as everywhere there is a great struggle for the soul of the Jew, that much that is old becomes shattered, and very little new is being built. But is it not true in the old home as well? That is the tragedy of the Jews in general today. Our generation or the generation after us will need to solve this problem: the question whether Judaism or the Jewish people can remain, or whether it is to be swallowed, whether a new Jewish form can be built on the ruins of the old structure or not. The question will probably become the sharpest in Jewish life, and America will be the great test of the Jewish strength. (...)

And we, the Jewish observers and dreamers of dreams also want an illusion. Possibly with time Canada may become a new, great Jewish centre. The possibilities are here. We need but to know how to use them. (...)

Question for Public Opinion
Reuben Brainin
Keneder Odler, June 8, 1914

The Jewish population in Canada numbers, in all probability, not less than 150,000, and in the light of the growing Canadian Jewish population as a cultural force, it is proper to consider the firm foundation of our future development in this country.

There are countries with fewer Jewish citizens than in Montreal alone, where they play a substantial political role, and participate in all areas of human activity, in science, art, and literature, trade, industry, finance, and other areas.

It is true that the Canadian Jewish settlement is still new and still young, but it is for that very reason that it must be raised to a higher purpose. (...) There is still what to do. It is still to be helped.

The Jewish community in Canada presents a complex political, social and economic problem. This problem is even more complicated, because it affects many other, and different areas.

World history, which has played complex and original experiments with the Jewish people for thousands of years makes with us an altogether new experiment in the wide and far Canada (...).

But the experiments on living people with a will are different from those on elements such as gold, which stay the same. (...) We make the experiment on ourselves. (...) The results depend on our own character.

When world history makes a new experiment with us, it transplants us onto new soil, in new political, social, economic and cultural conditions, in new material and intellectual spheres; world history receives the results which we ourselves produce.

The result depends upon how we conduct ourselves. (...) The Jewish religion tells: all the keys are with God. Only the keys of the awe of the Lord were given over to the hands of the human being, with other, simple words: we can decide to become saintly or wicked, angelic or diabolic in human shape.

A people, like an individual can become what he wishes to be and what he seeks to become. (...)

What is our desire in Canada? What is our ideal in this land? Do we have a higher ideal in Canada at all? Do we have a future here? Is anyone of us interested in these questions? (...) Did we come here only to earn a better or easier life, or only to enrich ourselves? How shall we teach generations to come? (...) Should we implant Jewish ideals in young brains and hearts? Who are our moral leaders, teachers, spokesmen of the Jewish race? (...)

These questions need to be debated by public opinion.

Editorial
Reuben Brainin
Presumed to be in the *Keneder Odler,* June 1914

The organization of the Jewish group in Canada and the development of a mass awareness suffers much from general conditions in the country.

We are absolutely dependent throughout the diaspora upon the dominating culture. Even in Russia, where the non-Jewish culture is at its beginnings, and the Jewish on the other hand is developed, nevertheless the Russian culture influences Jewish culture and literature.

In Canada, in particular, where Jewish culture is confused and Jewish construction has not yet begun, and our culture has not yet emerged; it does not yet have a day of existence in our literature, not even a photograph of our Canadian life.

What is the appearance of Canadian life, of the group who have become, through historical circumstances, the residents of Canada?

There is no homogeneous Canadian culture, neither cultural nor material. Culture here is, at best, being created behind the curtains of history. Some groups are seeking to seize new positions in the extensive, rich but as yet uncultivated country. The United States already counts many original poets, artists, thinkers and philosophers, but Canada scarcely has a representative in the world's spiritual culture.

Not only is Canada a new land, but Canada is torn in its blooming youth by nationalistic conflicts and religious strife and, like in all colonies, the conflicts are not internal but external, far from the metropolis, political and spiritual, far from being productive. No book has been written about the national question. No new harmonious slogan about the close relations between Protestant and Catholic philosophies. This lack of productivity of Christian culture in Canada has resulted in no deep problem having been strongly placed before the Canadian population. The Canadian people has not risen higher than its daily life and has not attempted to understand itself. It lives instinctively and no more.

Canadian life is temporarily disconnected and therefore more or less without content. This is reflected most by its press which is a nullity beyond the universal and civic. The term "the Canadian people" is virtually alien in the local press. There is no question of self-recognition on its pages. This is not mentioned, nor is it feared. There is a quiet spiritual anarchy which no one notices or wishes to note.

In the Canadian press (and there is no other Canadian literature in the country), no urgent cultural problem has been raised when the Canadian intelligentsia has left the people to their instinctive development. Thus the anarchy or the vacuum in the Jewish community becomes self evident.

It may appear that Jewish culture was not created yesterday, and is not dependant on other new cultures. There may be no great loss here. Does not Jewish culture have special Jewish problems, local and universal, to stir our nation or to freeze it, even when all about it is quiet?

But there are questions to pose to our complex exile history which is not created by us but by an ambient atmosphere. We are not the masters of our lives as long as we are passive to the creation of our culture, no more than the echo of the non-Jewish culture of the land where we reside.

Before we consider a Jewish public opinion in Canada, it would be proper to inquire whether there is a public opinion in Canada. How did it react to the tragedy of the *Empress of Ireland*? To the problem of unemployment from which our rich land suffers so inexplicably?

The land has not begun to develop to the state where the people could begin to determine its stand on demands, on aims, on victories, on an active history for the people of the nation, and for its Jewish people.

Canada and the Jewish Immigrants
Joseph Goodman
Presumed to be in *Keneder Odler* during World War I

The major cause of migration is economic. For the Slav and Ruthenian it was the sole cause. But Jewish migration bore another character. It was virtually never a question of the stomach; he did not come to the United States or Canada, as did the Irishman, because of a potato famine or an industrial crisis in his native land. The Jew came in flight, fleeing pogroms and the discriminatory legislation which robbed him of political and social equality. It was therefore sadder, more frightening, bitterer. The Jews play a more tragic role in the international drama of migration than other people.

The Jewish migrant came here in full knowledge that his economic condition may not improve, but because he wished to educate his children in freedom and equality. That has been the nature of our migration. What will it be after the war?

The Jewish population in the countries at war, estimated at 7,000,000, are economically ruined, hopeless and despairing, with no means of support (...) The very ruins of the war will provide employment for labourers, stone masons, steel workers — occupations in which the Jew is not represented.

Some half of them have become proletarians in recent years, but they have not been admitted to heavy industry; they have learned to make brushes, candy, cigars (...) The Jewish migration will also become a stomach migration; it will become much greater in extent than we can imagine.

Doubtless post-war immigration will become the greatest in our history, a colossal funeral march, and the sighs of thousands of unfortunates will resound over space. It will be greater than the wanderings which followed the first pogroms in 1882 when tens of thousands flooded the frontier villages of Germany and Austria.

Who could witness that frightful ruin of our people and not shed tears for the 30,000 homeless hungry, cold wanderers, crowding in filth in the shelters in Brody, and not share the feelings of Jeremiah as he penned the Lamentations?

We cannot forget that tragic historical moment. We must prepare and begin to think of our course of systematic action, remove the stones from the migrants' paths, lighten their tragic fate, wipe their tears.

Obligations of Canadian Jewry
A.M. Mandelbaum
Keneder Odler, October 13, 1915

(...)

Foremost is the looming problem of immigration (...) becoming more threatening as more elements are propagandising among Canadian workers that Jewish immigrants constitute competition for Canadian labour. (...) When a similar problem arose in the U.S., Jewish leaders mounted an effective campaignto the very White House.

What are Canadian Jews doing in the present situation? (...)

What is being done in Canada to disperse Jewish immigrants from the overcrowded cities?

In Canada we have tasted Jew hatred. There are no pogroms but we have experienced spiritual pogroms: the Quebec libel case, the ban on *shekhita* in Halifax, and other tragic events. Our national pride has been attacked.

These evils might have been avoided. We cannot force anyone to love us, but we can be on guard to defend our honour at all times throughout the country.

(...) Incontrovertibly, we need a central organization which will unite all the Jews in the dominion.

Such a force will be able to achieve what separate groups and parties cannot accomplish. It will determine who are worthy to speak in our name, to stand at the rudder of our affairs. Such a body will determine that such hostile developments as the Quebec City case are direct consequences of the ignorance of our Christian neighbours in regard to our aspirations, our efforts and our conditions in this country. We may decide that we must conduct tireless oral and written propaganda among Canadians to have them perceive us as a useful element and our immigrants as an enrichment for Canada.

I Protest
Rabbi Simon Glazer
Der Veg, Nov. 11, 1915

There are moments when the head must follow the heart, when the spirit conquers facts, when we lose control, when a secret force casts us beyond the horizon.(...)

I experienced such a moment when I read that some individuals want to convert a theatre here (the Gayety) next Sunday into a political market place. In spite of my firm decision to withdraw from all public activities, I find myself again in conflict. As I write these lines, [I cannot grasp what force (...) is driving me to protest, to appeal, to beg for pity, and to pour out the waves of my resentment.(...)]

[No Jewry in the world has to tell] the Great Powers what program they will have to implement on the day when the word peace will no longer be seen as shameful in the civilized world.

But our communal workers are crying out through the columns of the English press that they will show the way to England, Russia, France, Italy, Germany, Austria and Turkey. They do represent "three hundred Jewish organizations."

If this was happening only in the Jewish district, I would not enter the fray.

You who consider yourselves spokesmen for Canadian Jewry, who created a Jewry in Canada for you? Who built the institutions from whence you now draw honour? Who cleared up, washed and polished St. Dominique, Cadieux and other streets for you?

You would now push Jews to the abyss of anti-Semitism; where were you when *galut* Jews were dragged to police stations and stables during the night? When Jewish orphans were lost to us in Christian institutions?

Did you leaders of today ever try to crawl over shaky steps in tenements to look for a *minyan*? Go to seek out the lonely, the poor, the sick?(...) Did you ever try to feed your children on the wages paid by small synagogues on the Jews' streets? Did you ever sacrifice an hour of your repose for those who are truly the people?

No! (...) The Americanized, comfortable businessmen have built synagogues, schools and temples for you, have served you as ready-made Americanized youth, in order that you should hold for them outdated, meaningless sermons, and for this you are given powers and seats at the head table.

Be satisfied with your portion. You have taken for yourselves Sherbrooke

Street, Stanley Street and McGill Avenue. Keep them and enjoy each other.

Leave Cadieux Street and St. Dominique Street in peace. You have parted from your businesses? How can a divorcée live under one roof with her divorcé?

You have no right to take any political position on behalf of the million captured, exiled, usurped Jews!

This is no time to make any claims by any nation. The world is now bloodthirsty. The first lamb to cry "mehh!" will be devoured. When animals are loose in the forest and hungry, the shepherd may not whistle.

(…)Hold your Zionist convention, but leave general Jewish questions alone.

I advise you: you have hampered my work for years, but have stealthily adopted my ideas. I had decided to be silent.

But if you will dare next Sunday to touch my people, the poor victims who brought me up and fed me, from whence I grow, whose pain I feel, whose voice has now woken me up — you should know that my present action will be such that you yourselves will concede that the battle with you during the past decade will be but a preface. I am sending a copy of this protest to all Jewish newspapers in Canada.

The newly constituted Jewish 300, the self-appointed providers of the people's needs are coming to St. Urbain Street, to us — they are not convening in their district. They come to the people to be applauded by Jewish workers, peddlers, petty merchants. Why?

I believe that I do not need to ask their permission to address the Jews for whom I have sacrificed what may have been the best years of my life. On the contrary, I feel I should express myself. I have more right to do so, and I am less likely to be suspect.

I have refused to live on the salary from my people, or other such income. But I have never resigned my title or my sacred duty to serve my people at a moment of danger or to serve Jewish interests as I see them and when the time demands my views.

Convening a conference now is not my concern. If it were not harmful, I would not intervene. But my concern is aroused when I am certain that such a measure at this moment is dangerous and can bring misfortune upon many of our people.

When I fought for the observance of the Sabbath in Montreal and in Canada, for Talmud Torahs, for *kashrut,* for *shekhita* in Halifax, against anti-Semitism — these 300 persecuted me at every step. They could confuse matters by charging me with serving my personal interests.

Who among them could assert now that one word in any of these accusations is truthful?

Who could accuse me of speaking out against their dangerous steps in self interest? Who could claim that the Jewish people had mandated them to appear in the English press with a ready program for the world powers as to how they should deal with Ancient Israel?

[When the Jewish Federation calling for the controversial conference urged the community to hang out flags from their homes, I. Yampolsky was shocked by the bad taste of such gala displays during war time when so many Jews were being done to death on the front and behind the lines.]

A Jewish *simkha*? he asked as he cited one of the sacred books of the Jewish faith: God had been angry at the Jews when they sang His praise while so many Egyptians were dying at the Red Sea. 'The work of my hands are drowning in the sea, and you are singing the *shirah*!'

As the Year Ends
Rabbi Zvi Hirsch Cohen
Presumed to be in *Keneder Odler,* September 1913

In the business world it is customary to draw a balance for the concluding year and to consider plans for perfecting business during the coming year.

Some community institutions act similarly and issue public statements. I seek to do the same through the press articles to assist them in establishing a balance of our philanthropic and spiritual activities in this city and to note what more we can do.

It is with satisfaction that we look back upon the past year, the most fruitful since we have settled here. The old institutions have been expanded. Our Yiddish press, the *Odler* is now edited by Reuben Brainin, the leading thinker and author in Jewry, and the *Canadian Jewish Times* has passed into responsible hands.

The Baron de Hirsch Institute, the Talmud Torah, the *Kashrut* Committee, the Free Loan Society and the Zionist societies have been energetic. But we have not been content with the established bodies. We have created many new institutions that are excellent: the Ste. Agathe sanitarium with its substantial receipts, the Herzl Dispensary, the Young Men's Hebrew Association, the orphanage, the election of a Jewish alderman, the Jewish Fresh Air Fund, the *Kehillah* movement, the revival of the Hebrew Circle, *Ivriyah*, the Talmud Study Group uptown, Chevra Shass in the Shaar Hashomayim, the Young People's Auxiliary of the Talmud Torah, the planned north end branch of the Talmud Torah — they all indicate that Montreal Jews are beginning to sense their responsibility as citizens and as Jews to contribute and to create.

Every thinking Jew must be joyful and proud of these phenomena, but we cannot shut our eyes to what is still missing. Our orphanage must expand to receive all the Jewish orphans who are sheltered in Christian institutions, to be brought up under Jewish influence. Synagogue Jews must deal more seriously with religious problems. It is positive that Talmud seminaries in Russia and in *Eretz Israel* are being supported, but it is time for every sizable community to maintain its own *yeshiva*. Those who are permeated with the spirit of the Talmud must unite, must refresh this learning and must ensure that the Torah shall not be forgotten in Israel. The science of Israel must blossom in the free lands where our material condition is satisfactory as it blossomed in the days of Spain.

We regret that we must report that we cannot testify that a single restaurant in this city is kosher, and we have no answer to the few who inquire of us; and this is so because so few inquire. This is as true of sausages which are manufactured from unclean meat and are advertised as kosher. Observant Jews sell them to observant Jewish men and Jewish women. The rabbinical court here have made sacrifices to introduce kosher sausages, but the manufacturers noted that there is no greater demand for the kosher products than for others. They gave up and now they sell forbidden products as kosher, because of the Jews who publicly refuse to pay attention to our law. Further, there are the hypocrites who state that even foods which are produced under the supervision of the rabbis are also not truly kosher (...)

The Keneder Odler

The front page of the first edition of the *Keneder Odler*, August 30, 1907.
Canadian Jewish Congress National Archives.

THE FIRST YIDDISH NEWSPAPER in Canada, the *Keneder Odler* (The Canadian Eagle), appeared in Montreal in 1907. Its owner Hirsch Wolofsky, was a young Polish immigrant who had arrived in the city only seven years earlier, and who had cherished since adolescence the idea of one day creating a Yiddish paper. The opportunity to fulfil his dream finally came to him when a migration of unprecedented size arrived in the Quebec metropolis following the Russian revolution of 1905. In a very short time the number of potential readers for a Yiddish newspaper in Montreal multiplied and a whole community life in the process of defining itself was just waiting for a daring entrepreneur to echo its burgeoning activities in a daily local sheet.

The launching of the *Keneder Odler* was thus an immediate success, so great was the desire in the Jewish district to keep abreast of the latest developments in the city, in their own community and beyond. A whole generation of newly-arrived Yiddish-speaking immigrants who knew nothing of their new milieu learned the rudiments of Montreal and Canadian political life from the pages of this daily newspaper. Thanks to the *Keneder Odler*, Jewish philanthropic societies, *landsmanshaftn*, synagogues, recently established trade unions, and numerous small educational and cultural associations could finally reach their public. As well, newcomers affected by their expatriation and nostalgia for their country of origin could finally recognize in the pages of the Yiddish newspaper a certain familiar way of being and of reacting, as well as a language which reminded them of their *shtetl*, or now-remote native region.

Thanks to his newspaper, amply demonstrated in his memoirs published in 1946 under the title *Mayn Lebns Rayze*, Wolofsky became one of the most respected and significant leaders of Jewish Montreal. It should be understood that Wolofsky had founded his newspaper in the hope of contributing significantly to the development of its community, and to bring together energies dispersed by the worries of immigration and adaptation to a new environment. From the start, in the first issue published on August 30, 1907, the owner of the *Keneder Odler* delivered the message that the newspaper would defend Jewish interests in Canada, would seek to keep the flame of traditional Judaism alive in the country, would encourage the practice of philanthropy, and would support the idea of social justice for industrial workers. Wolofsky would be faithful to this ambitious program until the end of his career. In this sense, the first article, "To the Jews of Canada," is considered to be one of the founding texts of twentieth-century Montreal Jewish history by one of the most visionary individuals of the newly formed community.

The offices of the *Keneder Odler* in these first years was not a place where one thought calmly about the problems arising from the integration of a recently-arrived community. Quite the contrary, the exuberant instability caused by massive arrivals of immigrants and the population density of the Jewish district then located close to the port, contributed to an atmosphere of mob rule at any hour of the day in the editorial office of the newspaper. Many newcomers, who had left Eastern Europe without material resources and with nobody to truly rely on in Montreal, went almost immediately to express their grievances in the offices of the *Keneder Odler*. Under these conditions owner Hirsch Wolofsky, chief editorReuben Brainin, and the employees of the newspaper, unceasingly answered the questions and the requests of a multitude of individuals for whom the *Keneder Odler* was the only point of reliable reference in Montreal.

For decades the Yiddish daily acted as a signal post within the communal structure, making it possible to switch people onto the right track, and to provide some comfort to others who perhaps more cruelly felt the existential distress of immigration. This is the spirit captured in the humorous articles by journalist Isaac Yampolsky, who described the permanent agitation which reigned in the newspaper office of the *Keneder Odler*. The portrait of this environment would have remained incomplete without the articles by the journalist Baruch J. Goldstein, who clearly demonstrates that the Yiddish press of Montreal could also, on occasion, make room in the daily hurly-burly for great minds and literary men of high caliber. In this way, even in this backwater of the Yiddish-speaking diaspora, even in the very first hours of the great migration which was later to inundate the city, some individuals could be found to preserve the Eastern European Jewish intellectual tradition and to illustrate its deeper meanings.

To the Jews of Canada
Some words on the appearance of our newspaper and how it hopes to
secure a sure existence and the confidence of the public.
Our program.
The Editor of *Keneder Odler* (first issue)
August 30, 1907

When a newspaper appears it is customary for the publishers or the editors to issue a declaration of their intention and its direction. It is therefore the duty of the publishers of the *Keneder Odler* to state their fundamental principles, or the program which it will constantly maintain.

The press has recently become as vital a need in daily life as bread and water. A city without a newspaper is an impossibility nowadays. In the large cities consisting of various nationalities each colony has its newspaper, and we therefore observe German, French, Russian, Armenian, Polish, Arabic and even Chinese papers.

The Jews in Canada constitute a sufficient proportion to require several Jewish papers. But regrettably, hitherto, there has not been a Jewish paper. Jewish interests are neglected here. Jewish charity, brought forward as a model for the entire world, stands here at a very low level. Jewish citizenship plays a very minor part, for there is no newspaper to represent the interests of the Jewish citizens.

The *Keneder Odler* will faithfully represent Canadian Jewish interests.

The *Keneder Odler* will represent without fatigue that the Judaism which has maintained our unfortunate people in dark years of exile shall not be weakened.

That the education of Jewish children shall continue in the natural spirit and that its youth shall develop as a pride for our people.

The *Keneder Odler* aspires that Canada shall have the best Jewish charity institutions to serve as a model, and this newspaper will propagandize until this is realized.

There is no nation in the world which has as many who have suffered as much hardship as the Jews, as victims of pogroms and of anti-Semitic persecutions. The ill and the oppressed shall find comfort and support in the columns of the *Keneder Odler*.

Canada is a great, wealthy land. There is space here for hundreds of thousands of Jewish immigrants. On our side we shall strive to labour energetically to make Canada a new Jewish centre for our wandering brethren from Europe to find safety and freedom.

A proper Jewish education, national self-awareness, political security, and a true Jewish charity system and universal justice are the basic principles which the *Keneder Odler* shall not cease to promote.

Our columns will always be open to honest, non-sensational letters, reports, proposals and opinions.

The *Keneder Odler* will be the newspaper which will take the part of the Jewish worker. Union reports will be welcome and their just demands against the bosses will be supported by us.

We will give our best attention to daily events in Canada and the entire world, and Jewish news in particular.

We trust the *Keneder Odler* shall win the confidence of the public and that it will be supported by the Jewish population of Canada.

Respectfully, the publishers.

Brainin in the Editorial Room
B.J. Goldstein
Presumed to be in *Keneder Odler*, January 1910

It seemed to me that we were sitting with my friends in the old home under a broadly spreading tree, around a man seated on a stone as if he grew out of it, his face somewhat pale, covered by a transparent light cloud, his greying beard combed down, his friendly eyes glancing about him from time to time, with an old book in his hands telling of an ancient people.

He is reading from this book, and we, his thirsty pupils, swallow his words eagerly. As he turns the pages occasional sheets fall from the volume, but the book that he reads does not become more slim.

His words link in a chain of episodes, each stroke a new legend in the old-ever-new people. The eyes of the man grow into a smile at the anecdotes, as the smiles grow on our own lips, as the man on the height becomes more hopeful, as he reads the precise promise of prophecy; and a cloud covers his patriarchal features when a sad page comes to the fore.

The winter sun shines mildly on the street. Golden rays come down but do not reach us. For we are not sitting under a spreading tree but in the tiny office of the *Odler*, and we are friends who love to pore over the ancient book of our old people, who love to turn pages, to steep into the learning of the past, into the present and the future of the Jewish people, and Reuben Brainin was with us.

I have been with Brainin in hotel rooms, in different types of company, but I really saw him only in the narrow office of the *Odler*, separated from the outside world, surrounded by a spiritual thirst of the assembled metallic grey of the lines of type and the pages. Here the fleshly and external shell which covers the soul was shaken off, and there was revealed the ideal which is incorporated in the Brainin whom we can see in his lines and between his lines.

Brainin raises the curtain to reveal the poverty of the immigrants in Paris, and soon we are in cloudy Scandinavia. We are no longer in an office but are walking past Jewish stores and homes as we meet our brothers to whom we extend an inquiring *sholom aleikhem*, discuss storekeeping, and soon it is Jewish affairs that is our topic, Copenhagen Jewish schooling and the Jewish sentiments of the coming generations. We embrace Jews from Warsaw, Galicia and Russia; our room extends and we are in a broader Jewish world, Jews from home, long beloved images of many dimensions, dancing portraits.

He tells us that he has learned very much from his dispersed brothers and that there is much more to learn from them. He recalls Whitechapel with its Jewish wandering and trading adult community, but also its children, the citizens of tomorrow, with their plans and intentions.

Here he presented to us our brethren in Germany approaching us ever closer; our Jewish students, their faces cut by duelling swords, sitting at the *seder* table or reading Hebrew newspapers; our nationalistic groups at their work, demonstrating that the sweet voice of Jacob is to be heard in our syna-gogues but, when the time is for arrows and sword, Jacob no longer hides but strides forth to redeem the honour of his people.

We want this to remain constant; that Brainin sit so, that his pictures flow, and the old pages of his book of the antique Jewish people keep turning.

In the school he told the children happy tales. Suddenly he became a child sharing their minds and interests, at the same time he learned the measure of their Jewish spirit — and also of their teachers.

Our time is up. It is Yampolsky who ended it. Unwillingly we all rose from our seats and came down from that other world, uprooted from the green widely branched forest cast perforce outside the glass paned door which had until now served to separate sanctity from the profane, body from soul.

I could not forgive Yampolsky, and I spoke to him of it in later days. As we walked to the Anshei Sefard Talmud Torah we continued to converse. He narrated several humorous episodes on mixed marriages.

Counsel: The Monologue of a Visitor to the *Odler* Office
Isaac Yampolsky
Presumed to be in *Keneder Odler,* 1913

Have pity, Mr. Editor, on a Jewish soul, with some advice, or have your kindly and pious readers save me from my trouble which my woman brought on me.

The story of my history goes like this...

Two years ago my best friend, a playwright, dropped in after supper and asked me for a plot for a play he was about to write. I asked him, 'Do you have at least five dollars?' He answered. 'Where would I get five dollars?' I told him that if I knew I would go get them myself.

But my wife reminds me that the gentleman is our guest. 'Why do you not at least serve him some ginger ale or some peanuts?'

'You are right. Go down and get some.'

'You are not sick. You can go yourself.'

So I leave the two of them and go down to the small store next door. At the steps of the store I see a large package. Thinking heaven knows what is there, I open it and find several red apples, a package of Wissotzky tea, three bananas, a lemon and half a pound of sugar. I pushed it all in my pockets and entered the store. The young widow was not there, I waited for a while and was about to leave when I met her at the door (....)

'What is it you need?' she asked me. I told her but she said she did not have it.

I was about to leave, but she would not let me. She wanted to search me. Heaven only knows what she thought I had taken from her to impoverish her. I would not let her search me, 'So you must be a thief,' as she yelled out for a policeman. He came at once, found the treasure on me, took me to the police station. Thence they sent me, with all honours, from the court back to jail, sentenced to two years, no less, where I did not hear a word from wife or my friend.

You would think that was enough of God's punishment. But after sitting for eighteen months the director of the prison called me. As I stood in prison garb, head shorn, he told me, 'Your innocence has been proven and you are a free man.'

I was ready to run, the director held me back to tell me that the author of all my troubles had been my wife who had conspired with my playwright friend to jail me. He further revealed that my wife had gone off with the boarder of the widow next door. That night she caught a severe cold which developed into galloping consumption. In the sanatorium she called for a rabbi before her passing, but the man who came was a Jewish convert to the Church, a priest who heard her confession.

My playwright friend was on his way to Chicago in the sleeping car which also carried the widow who had managed the little store next door to me, now also on her way to her sister in Chicago; they had been living together since. He faced her in her apartment prepared to kill her.

As she pleaded for mercy she confessed that she had been in love with me since she first saw me, and she had taken part in the conspiracy to ensure I would be divorced. She had told her story to the playwright who threatened to reveal all and forced her into prostitution with him.

Her story awakened strong love in me towards her — just when the playwright entered and, they quarrelled violently.

To bring Yampolsky's column to an end before the editor expired, the visitor came to his point. He needed titles for a serial novel which he was writing of his life for the newspapers, and for a play with music for the Yiddish stage. He has thought of "The Beautiful Widow" and "The False Wife".

Brainin was to advise which of the titles was for his novel, and which for the musical play he should use. (....)

A Day in the Editor's Office
Isaac Yampolsky
Keneder Odler, April 3, 1913

May God help anyone who is punished for being jealous of an editor by endowing him with corns on each of his fingers so that he will be unable to take a pen in hand.

God helped me and I became a member of the editorial staff; that is, I sit behind the editor's shoulders and make sure that the waste paper basket does not overflow and bring the editor back to life when he faints.

I want to tell you of only one day in his life. You will lose your appetite to be an editor.

Just imagine him sitting, his eyes buried deeply in his desk writing. I am beside him whistling a melody. Behind the door the reporters scribble quietly, peacefully. Suddenly a knock on the door and, before both call 'come in,' a woman grows up at our side, with child at her hand and says to us,

'Are you the editor?'

'Sit down,' he said to her. 'What can I do for you?'

'I am asking you to put him in the papers and bury him deep, my husband, I mean. He deserted me two years ago because I was yelling at him, he said. Do I yell? It is only my habit. I speak loudly.'

'What can I do for you?' the editor begged.

'What do you mean? He doesn't support me,' she yells.

'But there is the court house.'

'He has disappeared, and the devil knows where he is.'

'So go to the Baron de Hirsch Committee.'

'They have no God in their heart.'

'There is no way I can help you,' the editor said, out of patience, and taking to writing.

'At least you can write him up', she says, without moving from where she is.

'Do you have a photograph of your husband?' I asked.

'I have two.'

'Keep one and we will put the other one with the Missing Husbands.'

She thanked me and the editor thanked me for ridding him of her.

When I came back I found another nuisance plaguing the editor for the address of the rabbi of his *shtetl*.

'I don't know your town and don't have the address of its rabbi,' the editor said.

'I am trying to get rid of my plague.'

I tried to be helpful, I think our *shoykhet* is from your town. Here is his address. Go to him quickly before he is off to the slaughterhouse.

Before he is out the three typesetters rush in, ink-smudged noses and sleeves rolled up like robbers. Manuscripts, please. The machines are idle.

'Just a moment, take what I have ready. By the time you have done this, I will finish the rest.'

They are no sooner out when an important visitor who cannot be so easily dismissed comes in. He has written a report of a masquerade ball that his society had sponsored.

'I don't like to trouble you,' he said sitting down generously, 'but why did you allow my report to pass with a mistake, with a 'yes' instead of a 'no'?'

'It was the proofreader who missed it.'

'Why do your articles always come out right and my report has an error?'

I interrupt him, 'Your handwriting is crooked.'

'I always write at an angle.'

'Our proof reader is also slant-eyed.'

The editor is panicky. I told him I would stand at the door and tell all comers that he is not well today. I had not moved an inch when a cylinder with a beard barged in, a passing reverend.

'What is it that you want?'

'I just want to get to know you. I will speak in a synagogue on Sabbath, so I'd like you to write something about me.'

The editor promised and said good-bye to him.

The next visitor was the choirmaster of the *Welcoming of the Bride Society* arranging a concert during the weekend, here to invite the editor to the event, after he would write an editorial on the worthy cause. I suggested an advertisement instead.

I return to the office and see the editor writing feverishly. The pen bends under the speed and races like a fire. If anybody will interrupt him I will throw him down the steps head first. I enjoy watching him write and I am jealous of his fluidity and currency. It is a great matter: a man like any other man writes thought after thought and the paper is filled with thoughts. It is taken downstairs and the written thoughts are printed in thousands of papers and the tens of thousands of readers tell them to each other.

I take up my pen and also write. We both write. Writing is like a milk cow. As long as the milk comes, we milk. When the milk stops coming, we milk it anyway.

'Take it downstairs, please. I don't want to see their faces.'

I met the three of them at the door.

The editor lights a cigar: I a cigarette. He begins to plan the next day's paper. But a young man appears with a naive poem which he reads to the editor; he hints he has many more at home — when the editor promises to take the first poem. I whisper to him that the editor is a jealous man who throws good poems from new writers into the basket.

After he leaves the editor reminds me, 'Our Jews are indeed the people of the book.'

The telephone rings. 'You wrote in your paper that I caught a thief in my store and that he split my head.'

'And he did not split your tongue?'

As we were putting our coats on he said, 'You can go crazy here.'

'On the contrary, it is cheerful here.'

At the door we come to face with a newcomer who has written an article on prostitution and socialism; he was proud of his handwriting.

'Do you read Yiddish papers?'

'I can only write.'

'Do you read books?'

'No, but, I write very well.'

The editor glanced at the manuscript and returned it. 'It is written on both sides of the paper. When we give it to the printer it has to be written on one side. You as a beginner wrote it on the side that is not to be written on.'

'But I do have talent, don't I?'

'You will work your way in,' we tell him and he walks away happy.

We were happier having survived a day in the editorial office.

On the Editor's Office
Isaac Yampolsky
presumed to be in *Keneder Odler,* 1914

I have clarified in my notes to my friend, who has for some time left me free, but now has come to miss me and visited me in the editorial room, that:

A Jewish editorial is a community centre, a day and night chapel populated by all sorts of people, and the editor must be there all day and all night functioning as judge, rabbi, rebbe, advocate, sustainer of life, supporter of those failing, healer of the sick, liberator of the imprisoned, the man of much power, the friend of the Jews, counsel, doctor, psychiatrist, defender of children and of women, philanthropist, executive, immigration officer, social worker, intercessor, procurator, public defender, pleader, collector, family defender, protector of the humiliated, collector for the needy and persecuted, guarantor of Talmud Torahs, employment agent, loan commissioner, protector of women, children and of workers and visitor of the sick.

The editor must hear everyone patiently, every bitter heart, everyone's troubles, all complex issues and cases which Jews have with the world. No one considers when the editor will do his work, when he will write what he is obliged to, when he will read the mountains of manuscripts and books which arrive daily at his desk which he is obliged to review. I am jealous of the traditional 'Good Jews' who could besmear the angels in the heavens — but since your servant is not a good Jew, I must, by virtue of our manifold sins, be my personal self; my brain and effort and pen what I have to say and print.

Regardless of all this, I deeply enjoy the visit of my friend. Whoever comes to me, I become aware that he needs me and the newspaper. It is only when he needs us; otherwise he would never see us, directly or indirectly.

A rich man once told a poor Greek philosopher, 'What good is your philosophy, I am greater than you, because you come to me for a loan, but I never have occasion to come to you.' The philosopher responded, 'I come to you for what I need, and you respond. But you never come to me for the wisdom which you lack, but are unaware of your need.'

My friend comes to me, and gives me pleasure. He never comes empty-handed; sometimes it is with simple news from the city, all of which he hands to me, leaving nothing for himself. Indeed he sometimes adds some of his own piquant decoration to his factual report, and tries hard to interest me, so that I may hear him.

Where does he find the interesting city news? That is his own secret, from the first source, before anyone else, and more than anyone else, and before telling it to anyone else, to a good friend. When he feels that I have no interest in those public affairs, he tells me an ancient, half baked tale or fresh tale. Is there anyone who is not a customer for a fine sharp Jewish joke?

But when my friend notices that I was not moved by his wit — he had not drawn a laugh or even a smile from me — he favours me with some good counsel, with friendly advice on how to write my sinful editorial so that the goat remains whole and the wolf sated, that both sides are satisfied, both right and left, that it burns like fire and is cold like ice. Sensing his failure, he hands me a severe sentence, preaches some morality and warning; do not touch this, nor the other; we need not laugh at all costs, for in our hearts we despise them all; the rich and powerful, men of family and strategy are not being provoked when they call light night and the editorialist needs to proclaim it is night, absolutely. These superior ones having declared the profane sacred, the editorialist must declare that it is the purest of the immaculate. If those leaders are misleaders, the editor must call to all his readers; flock of sacred ones, follow the just shepherd with eyes shut, even in pain, he is your philanthropist, your protector and your guide.

In short my friend often lectures me in editing, and — why deny it to you and to myself? — he is my teacher and rabbi, yet he is dissatisfied with me, this poor disobedient pupil.

'I see you will never cease to be the greenhorn, never become the American, the Canadian wise man.' Apparently, he is not wrong.

Yesterday he visited me in the editorial room, after an absence. I had not seen him for some time. 'What is new, my Jewish friend?'

Troubles, pains; debts, complications. His face was very sad.

'Why so downcast? You are accustomed to this after time and circumstances; now your nose is low. The Jewish God still lives and he does not forget his people Israel.'

'But he has forgotten me,' my friend contradicted me. 'Yet I have not asked for much. Does a Jew need millions? I asked but twenty thousand dollars. Does a Jew need ten suits? I would have been satisfied with two or three; thirty underthings? Two or three would do me, a half dozen shirts, a gold watch.'

'And what would you do with such riches?'

'I would wish but one thing, to be on the *Empress of Ireland* and sink with my treasure and escape with one shirt.'

'And what would become of your twenty thousand dollars and your three suits, and your half dozen shirts, if you escaped with one shirt?'

'I would at least be able to speak of one shirt. As it is I do not have even this.'

— My poor friend.

Reuben Brainin

Writer Reuben Brainin was invited by Hirsch Wolofsky
to become the editor of the *Keneder Odler*.
From *The Jew in Canada*, 1926.

REUBEN BRAININ was undoubtedly, until his departure for New York around 1917, the greatest among the Jewish intellectuals who resided in Montreal. His breadth of spirit and his exceptional level of education also made of him, alas, an isolated and misunderstood man within a Jewish community populated almost exclusively with poor immigrants coming from the culture of the *shtetl*. Born in Lyady in Bielorussia in 1862 and raised within a traditional Jewish religious milieu, Brainin had lived in Vienna during his youth. There he came into profound contact with Western literary culture and participated in the great intellectual debates surrounding Jewish modernity. During these years he earned an enviable reputation as a Hebraic writer and was influential in European progressive Jewish circles. At the same time, Brainin also wrote regularly on parallel topics for the best-known Eastern European Yiddish newspapers.

In 1909, after a brilliant European career devoted to the field of letters, Brainin decided to emigrate to the United States. In the New World, where no Yiddish intellectual current yet existed, the Jews of the Diaspora did not attach as much importance to the aspects of the spirit as their counterparts in Europe. In this context Brainin no longer found the institutional support on which he had been able to count on in central Europe, and had to agree to work for a Jewish press whose readership was composed primarily of recent and still unacculturated immigrants. This explains why, in 1912, Brainin became, at Hirsch Wolofsky's invitation, the head of the *Keneder Odler*. The newspaper, founded five years earlier, (and for which Brainin became the fifth writer at its head), had a readership composed almost exclusively of penniless refugees who had fled the autocratic Russian regime. It served a community that was still in its infnancy.

The arrival of Brainin in Montreal would constitute an unhoped-for starting point for those few immigrants who were attempting to bring an embryo of Jewish artistic and intellectual life to the city. Fifty years old at the time of his arrival in 1912, Brainin indeed had the stature and prestige necessary to inspire the community towards the foundation of the first cultural institutions: a public library, Yiddish secular schools, circles devoted to popular education, and even Yiddish literary salons. Brainin also lent his prestige to the promotion of the interests of the many Jewish workers in Montreal. He defended their right to decent living conditions and organization within trade union structures. A conflict developed, however, between Brainin and Wolofsky, his employer. Its principal cause was the management of community affairs, and among them the creation of the Canadian Jewish Congress, the creation of the Jewish Public Library and the educational institutions which had by then started to appear in the city. Brainin, whose personality is amply described by M.Z.R. Frank in two articles, suffered greatly living in a milieu located on the margin of the great intellectual centres, where he was not able to fully use his talents.

The rupture between Brainin and the *Keneder Odler* led to Brainin publishing a competing Yiddish newspaper in Montreal on September 1915 called *Der Veg*. It was far more literary than the *Keneder Odler*, and it aspired to be a place of ideological reflection on major contemporary Jewish problems. *Der Veg* lasted only two years and its demise marked the departure of Brainin from Montreal. He returned to New York in 1919 to assume the editorship of *Ha-Toren*, a new weekly Hebrew-language publication. Thereafter, he returned only sporadically to Montreal. The departure of Brainin was also, in a sense, the symbol of a rupture between the Yiddish-speaking Montreal immigrant world and the universe of the Diaspora installed in the large cultural capitals of Europe at that time — Vienna, Paris, Berlin, and, St. Petersburg. The literary and erudite environment which came into being in Montreal would take different paths from those which Brainin had hoped for, and it was only established at last between the two wars, after a long period of cultural and community maturation.

Brainin's impatience regarding the situation which prevailed in Montreal before World War I is well reflected in an article translated by David Rome, whose origin is not certain, but which is presumed to belong to the sphere of personal writings of this major intellectual. It is difficult to imagine that Brainin would choose to publish such disagreeable reflections about the Montreal Jewish public in 1914 in the *Keneder Odler*, at a time when he was obliged, by virtue of his position, to express a certain attachment to his adopted city and its Yiddish-speaking inhabitants. Although the date is not known with certainty, one easily perceives that it is a text expressing the impotence felt by its author, as well as an emotional pain partly alleviated by his departure from the city. One also sees a vividly-coloured profile of the profound clash between the Yiddish and Hebrew literary and cultural traditions. Both traditions were in the process of emerging out of the nineteenth century, and were destined to battle on all fronts to exert their predominance within the Jewish world. Brainin was soon to note bitterly that in Montreal, in the middle of the large Yiddish-speaking migration, Hebrew cultural nationalism fought with unequal weapons and had no chance to impose its dominance.

R. Brainin on the Jewish Masses
Reuben Brainin
Presumed to be in *Keneder Odler*, no date

There is no mass of people in the world as intelligently prepared for sacrifices and for ideal causes as the Jewish masses.

In order to love the Jewish people and to learn to believe in its ability to live and create its autonomous existence, it is essential to penetrate into the lives of our poor brothers, our workers, our tradesmen, our proletarians, our petty merchants in their sad, depressive lives. Yet, how many bright spots there are there, how much spiritual riches there are within their poverty, how many healthy seeds of development are to be found on these poor Jewish streets!

I do have occasion to spend some summer months in various resorts in the proximity of wealthy Russian Jews, to observe their relations with each other and to enter their poor world of emotions and ideas. In their company I feel myself in the *tohu bohu* of people with no heavens above their heads or ground under their feet, people torn from their nation, from their past, with no dreams of future. As a writer among them, I feel afloat in an abyss, a peculiar creature in my own eyes.

As a writer my duty is to hold a mirror up to all classes of my people, to show all the weaknesses and flaws, the wounds and ills that plague the poor and the workers as well as the rich and the powerful.

At this point I direct myself to our poor, pale and powerless intelligentsia, to evoke their energy, faith and courage, and to appreciate that they live and work out of true love for our poor brethren, intimately bound with the Jewish masses.

We must stand in the midst of their life, and we must turn over all that we possess — all that is luminous, aware, cultured, Jewish educated — to them voluntarily, with pleasure. By frequenting them we will become the richer, and vitally more powerful.

Ask not the doctor; ask the patient. I, too, was torn for many years from the Jewish masses and lived in a universe of abstractions and theory, a world of shadows without reality, without action, a world of peelings, without seed.

Five years ago I went to Hamburg to study the migration movement. For weeks I lived the lives of immigrants day and night, shared their troubles.

I was newly born; I recognized my unfortunate brothers and their true qualities and faults. I realized that our literature, the art and dreams of our future are justified only when they are nourished on our true life, the life of our Jewish masses.

What to do? ('Sketch')
Reuben Brainin
Keneder Odler, April 15, 1909

What to do? You ask me to write you, but I do not know if I can describe what I wish, what I really want to tell you, as one tells a friend. Somehow the pouring out of my heart to a friend does not come in words or in a letter; I am not sure you will understand me completely. You are a little distant from our places, and in the meantime all has changed and become other.

I sometimes sit for long with my thoughts, no one to address a word; everyone has his bundle, his problems and worries and is carried away in his own issues.

There is nothing to do, and I have no idea where I should turn. Every moment a new thought is born, a new plan, a new project. But instantaneously it becomes clear that they are all silly dreams and fantasies. (...) I seek a purpose, an aim in life. Life is indeed aimless, a burden, a nightmare, a "bluff". So, why do I live? Why do others live?

So the hours drag on, the days, the months. Life is a sort of mud, stagnant, [as a liberation movement].

I want to flee to Palestine, to become a simple worker there, to fight for our future, for the national independence of our people. At such a moment, it seems to me that a great hour has come, with Turkey free; we the young Jews can create great things in the land of Israel. Twenty-five years ago, there were *biluim* and now has come the time for another sort of pioneers. I would run barefoot to the Holy Land, to this sacred task. At such a moment I look at the young people in our *shtetlekh* and ask, what are they doing here? Who needs them here, and whom do they need? Why are they not going to our old homeland where a new life can be started? Where every drop of their perspiration can serve coming generations?

Yet at such moments of "historical wonderment" another, a contrary thought occurs to me. Why not America, why not "make" a living in America, with the million Jews in New York, with advancing Jewish culture there, in Yiddish, where intelligent people, leaders, are needed; establish a Jewish paper in that city, reform the Yiddish theatre, promote true Jewish art?

I no sooner form this thought than another pushes it away: to remain in the *shtetl*, become a teacher. How can I desert my oppressed poor brethren who are being deprived of all their old homes in darkness, without a proper teacher for the next generation who will grow wild with no education or ideals?

And then I think: can I return to Switzerland, to Germany? My recent years were passed in community work, mostly in propaganda pamphlets. I have not even read much, except a little fiction that has come to hand. So I decide to begin to study. I am prepared to return to Switzerland, to Paris to study. No, I must make something of myself before I begin to teach, to become a bearer of culture. I must know something myself, and at such a moment I see myself drawn with all my powers to study.

But this only a brief moment. Questions and doubts as to what to study, without preliminary certificates, without money, without the skills to resort to the dry books essential for study. And, at best, what after I have studied? How many of my doctor friends who are still without knowledge or skill or employment, passing their lives with no purpose. Is a diploma necessary?

But what to do? Perhaps I should devote myself to literature. My talents are no lesser than all my friends who have become well-known and my knowledge greater and purer. So I begin to write dramas, sketches, short stories, and it seems that they are not bad, at least not worse than others that now appear; sometimes better, more profound, more artistic.

The trouble is that I begin to write and do not finish. I remain at the beginning, for as I enter the theme there comes the bitter question: who will publish it, who is the expert in purely artistic matters? Who will sponsor it? For I know that without it the written word will not enter the "Temple of the Muse." I know that when one enters the field of literature one must rub shoulders with a "great" writer, to be a sort of *khusid* with a *rebbe*, and I do not know how one does this.

Young Jewish Criminals in Montreal
Reuben Brainin
Keneder Odler, February 26, 1913

The judge stated that] (…) Jewish delinquents are no more or less numerous than others.

But the nature of their delinquency is different from the French Canadian or English children. They are generally more skillful and efficient. They commit their crimes with greater intelligence.

Jewish delinquents generally do not attend schools or *Talmud Torahs*. They are idle street children, mostly children of immigrant parents from Russia, Galicia, and Romania (…)who have assimilated with the street culture here and speak English well.

(…)In his view the Jewish children are not corrupt by nature. They are ignorant, living in a bad environment, who never heard a kindly word from teachers, parents or preachers. In some cases parents are directly responsible for the crimes of their children. Some force their children to bring money home and, if these children cannot earn such money, they steal. They generally turn in stolen moneys and articles to their parents who do not care about the source of these funds.

(…)The children are brought before the judges, largely on charges of stealing from jewellery stores or picking pockets,(…) they are international, not differentiating between Jews or Christians.

They are also induced to crime to provide them with cigarettes and with tickets to movies.

(…) If the children cannot usefully be returned to the care of their parents, they are sent to reform schools who often influence the children for good. When this is observed in the reform schools, the children are returned to their homes before the conclusion of the term of sentence.

Anti-Semitism and its Causes
Reuben Brainin
Keneder Odler, January 11, 1914

Last Wednesday distinguished Jewish citizens discussed anti-Semitism in the Shaar Hashomayim synagogue. The discussion evoked contrary opinions.

In truth this question should have been discussed in Christian circles, for Jew-hatred is their illness, their error, their fault, not ours.

But it is a good thing that our prominent co-religionists are giving attention to this consideration because it leads to Jewish awareness. (…)

But it seems that not all participants in the Shaar Hashomayim had considered anti-Semitism from all sides or had dealt with it deeply or soundly.

It was Clarence I. de Sola who approached the problem most deeply, but even so only in part; not even he had delved to its final consequences.

There was in all the discussions — (and particularly in the thinking of Mr. Michael Hirsch) — one basic error, as noted by the English *Gazette* and by many in the audience: the cause of anti-Semitism lies not in the non-Jewish world, but in us alone.

And this is a basic error.

I wish to recall incidentally that Abe Cahan, in his famed Montreal speech found the seeds of anti-Semitism outside Judaism, within Russian despotism. When despotism in Russia would be shattered, anti-Semitism would altogether disappear, in one morning.

But this approach is also basically flawed.

For anti-Semitism exists and has struck deep roots in lands where despotism has faded long ago. All the more: there are freethinkers, revolutionaries who have liberated themselves from prejudices and other superstitions but cannot free themselves of anti-Semitic sentiments and approaches.

In truth the sentiments on anti-Semitism expressed in the synagogue, like the opinions heard from Abe Cahan on this matter, were one-sided and outdated by several decades.

Meanwhile, the literature on the causes of anti-Semitism has grown into a considerable international body. The historical, psychological and social sciences, anthropology and political movements have accumulated a rich storehouse of experience, documentation and facts that shed a light and explain anti-Semitism in various countries and long epochs from many sides.

We now know that this vice cannot be explained by one cause. It has roots in religion, racism, economics, society and politics, and in many other causes.

In some lands or epochs, the religious motives are stronger; in other areas and at other times we sense economic and social forces at work; at each time and in all countries anti-Semitism is fed by different sources. The external mask of anti-Semitism alters with time and according to countries, but it is innately the same: the hatred of the strong toward the weak, of the many for the few, of the native for the alien, the newly arrived; of the victor for the defeated.

The hatred of us is inherited; it is our heritage from the nations, the heritage of millennia, it is a blind instinct seeking to justify many ends.

German anti-Semites have created a scientific literature which attempts to justify their hatred of us by religious history, by anthropology, the race problem, sociology, cultural history, national psychology.

Hatred of us is the Aryan peoples' blind fear of the Semitic, of the Jewish spirit. We are the bone in their throat: we cannot be swallowed and we cannot be spit out. Our culture is too strong, our spirit and national awareness too clean, too deep, too unquestionable, too clear, too unassimilable to disappear. Their cultural stomach is too weak to swallow it and to digest it. Too hard a bite.

They hate us not because of our faults but because of our virtues, abilities, because we have heart and soul. They could forgive us for our faults, but not for our virtues.

Unconsciously they cannot forgive us for having given them a god, a god who was a Jew, a religion of love which is alien to their spirit and to their bellicose instincts.

We know that the cause of anti-Semitism lies not in us but in them, because we are socialists, revolutionaries, awakeners, restless spirits.

And they hate us because we are capitalists, exploiters, blood suckers, superstitious religious fanatics or some because we are atheists, because we disturb religious sentiments, because we are sacrilegious, faithless; because we are unclean, stingy, because money is our soul, or because we live ostentatiously, beyond our means, luxuriously, in riches and glory. They cannot tolerate us because we are not cultured enough, and others because we are too educated in culture.

They hate us because we are aggressive, because we lower ourselves, and some because we are too proud, too self-confident, because we are too aware of ourselves, our great men, our geniuses. Some persecute because they do not know our history and our religion; others because they know our sages and our faith all too well.

Because we know the psychology of anti-Semitism much better than we did a generation ago, our response must be altogether different than those who learned it long ago.

We shall speak of it again.

Reuben Brainin
Presumed to be from *Brainin's Diary,*
February, 1914

On this Purim night of my fifty-second birthday I make an accounting of my life; I summarize my life and efforts and aspirations; I compare my will and my abilities, my past and my future, and I sense a secret hand ruling my fate.

I deeply regret that several years ago I was forced to leave my literary Hebrew work, and I do not even publish what I write in Hebrew. I weep in secret that I have distanced myself from Europe and my work in Hebrew literature there. I am aware of the great ocean between me and my past there, and I cannot see any possibility of returning to my first work there. Even the new Hebrew authors are alien to me, although they are dear and beloved to me for their special simplicity and their perspicacity.

For the past two years I have limited my literary work to the *Odler.* Every day I write various Yiddish essays, many of them in my view not without true literary value. Since I became editor I have composed some seven hundred literary pieces on nations and on men, on current affairs, on authors and on literature, on the mysteries of life, on social movements and on science, recollections, analyses on well known public figures, on economics and on the problems of Judaism and on the Jewish questions.

But none of these works are of value to me because they are in Yiddish and not in Hebrew. In truth, I can say that, now that they have been written, it is as if they had not been written.

I am dust in the literature of Hebrew; but much more so since I am writing in the Yiddish press of Canada, for who are my readers? Suffice it that I write in Yiddish to which my soul is not bound; but the newspaper I am editing has no wide circulation for it is not widely distributed in the U.S. and only a few copies reach Europe, and most of my literary essays are written only for myself.

This is my greatest punishment for the sins which I have sinned and also for the sins which I have not sinned.

I flagellate my body for having been sold to the Yiddish press, for just now I cannot see my bones being brought out of Egypt.

During the two years that my family and I have been in Canada I have worked more than during a decade in Europe, and I do not have a free minute, for my hours are devoted to Montreal community service. All Jewish affairs, all social activities, all institutions rest on my shoulders. I have established new services in the community. Vision has left me. The Hebrew author has been transformed into a community worker; I changed my golden cane into copper pennies.

By constitution I am only a writer and I never sought to be more than a writer, for literature is dearer to me than all the delights of the universe. My present work has convinced me that I have no business with wild people or cripples irremediably devoured by love of money or of honours.

The residents of Canada are the remnants of the generation of the flood. There can be no bridge or point of juncture between our worlds, and it is not Brainin the author who is attracted to fiery community service but another Brainin, a stranger to the earlier Brainin.

I dream all day and all night of literature, philosophy and science. This is my inner world, and community work with all its breadth and detailing has never searched me out in the hidden interstices of my spirit and in the soul of my soul.

I am a drowning man in an ocean of pettiness and my Yiddish literary work is only an instrument to my public service.

My life in Canada is at the mercy of all earners; the editor's chamber is open to the near and the distant, to all complaints and demands, to every child and every plaintiff, to the crippled, the stupid and to minors — all pleading for support and help, all robbing me of my time and my energies. Now that I am lost, I admit that I am lost. Resignedly I give them my hours and my strength. I have nothing left for Hebrew literature.

I am not happy for my gift to all passers by, to all the dispirited and embittered souls. I am disposing of my life and soul. I treasure an hour of Hebrew literature above all the days I have been giving to community service in Canada for which all are grateful to me and appreciate. I despise my public service.

In spite of all that is within me, to the embitterment of my spirit I have become a sort of leader, a sort of spokesman for Canadian Jews whose eyes are lifted to me for my words and my judgements.

That is defeat and descent of the soul for Brainin the author.

Here I am writing in the *Odler* on the bitter truth about the community; I fight its strongmen leadership, its impertinent representatives. Many find strength and heroism, greatness and glory here. But I regret that I have ceased to fight against the market that has occupied the heart of the Hebrew people, its exilic condition; that I have ceased to pronounce the truth about the national condition from every elevated pulpit and I am forced to fight in a narrow circle against heroes whom I despise. Even if I secure triumph against them it will give me no satisfaction.

Life Among the Common Folk
Reuben Brainin
presumed to be in *Der Veg,* date unknown

Spiritual and moral threads have woven me to my readers. During these three years I have had daily proof that it is possible to influence and to do good through the printed word when it is serious and sincere.

A Jewish paper, when it is dignified and it maintains its level, has the significance of a parliament, a people's university.

I have come to love the young Jewish community where fate has cast me. I am free to refer to the Talmudic expression, at first by force, finally by will.

For I believe in the future and in the possibilities of development in the Jewish settlement in Canada. It is possible to create much here on new foundations; there are broad fields to sow.

During the past ten months I was robbed of the possibility of speaking daily to the Jewish public. As a Jewish optimist I can now say all that God does is for the best. I have learned much during this time, not only from books, but even more from the first source, from life itself. I came in closer touch, in more immediate touch with the people, with their material and spiritual needs, their suffering in their struggles; I have come closer to the ever fresh, even if hidden, sources of idealism and readiness to sacrifice, which flow in the souls, the true people's soul. I have gotten to know the better part of our young people, our working people; their thirst for knowledge, their potential for growth, being with them downtown, not as a writer, a journalist. As our proverb has it, ask not the doctor, ask the patient. On my own body, I learned the effectiveness of public medicine, the printed word. This has been the vivisection of my own soul.

On Brainin & Kaufman

M.Z.R. Frank

Presumed to be in *Ha Doar,* no date

The true founder of the Jewish Public Library and Jewish People's University, its living spirit, was Kaufman, who had Brainin named as its president. He introduced Brainin into its activities and its atmosphere, which in reality were alien to Brainin.

Kaufman was a people's man in all his senses. Indeed his opponents from the left, within his *Poale Zion* group and outside it suspected his hebraism, but he loved his mother language deeply as in his very being and training. I recall his teaching us Yiddish folk songs and Yiddish Chassidic songs even in Jerusalem where most of his conversation and his affairs were in Hebrew and about Hebrew. He loved Yiddish in all its manifestations and revelations.

Brainin was different. His years in Vienna and in Berlin had ruined and Germanized his Yiddish speech. His service as editor of a Yiddish newspaper introduced him into the maze of petty matters such as *kashrut* and city elections where all was confusion for him, but he could not avoid seeking to elevate public affairs to greater heights.

Indeed during Brainin's first months in Montreal the public elevated him to spokesman on grave matters. He was the Berliner for the ignorant who came to touch the fringes of his garments as he appeared at important public demonstrations. Kaufman saw the light in the Brainin humanity, the practical community maker. In the library he bridged the abyss between refined Brainin and the men of the people hungry for creative enlightenment, many of them close to the *Poale Zion.* Brainin attended meetings of the library, busied himself with elections and campaigns and committees and teaching the people.

It is doubtful whether anyone but Kaufman could have convinced him to join the men of the *landsmanshaften* and the Labour Zionist movement.

The school which Shloimeh Wiseman came to lead after Kaufman left Canada is not only representative, but is the best of them. Kaufman shone over it, gave it direction and standards, influenced its atmosphere and inspired its activities through all their difficulties.

On R. Brainin and Clarence de Sola
M.Z.R. Frank
Presumed to be in *Keneder Odler,* July 1914

His likeness which I saw there for the first time has remained with me; I could not forget his dark cape, his black beard, his purple necktie, the image of an energetic man of faith and directness; above all, the refined lines of his face, his noble eyes. It was a new name for me; I had not read a line of his. But his portrait touched me more deeply than those other Hebrew writers whom I knew and loved.

(...) As a child in the Hebrew school in my *shtetl* I was deeply impressed by the clear pure words of Reuben Brainin — and by his beautiful, dignified beard. I would pore over his photographs and see a Jewish scholar, a sage, an erudite — Torah and wisdom together.

The aesthetics about the man extended to all he touched. Later I came across some numbers of his *Hadror* which reached us from New York. I was impressed by their graphic beauty which was not to be found in other Hebrew periodicals of the time.

[Soon young Frank met Brainin in the office of the *Odler*, for an opinion on Frank's *Fantasia*:]

(...) He was more beautiful than the postcard which I had carried in my mind. His hair was not all black, with a touch of time which was also reflected in his eyes and in their dreams, wondrously beautiful. He was more masculine than on the card; there was less of the softness in his face which testified to weakness, and his eyes and movements spoke of vitality and mobility. His voice was hearty and heartening, the movements of his hands and body were fine and gentle, his dress neat; at the time he was wearing a summer suit.

Brainin was very short-sighted. When he rose to speak from the platform he would look very closely at his watch, so closely that it seemed to touch the pupils of his eyes. But I never saw him wear glasses, and I am sure that no one else ever did either. In any other man such vanity would arouse a smile, but there was no such temptation with Brainin.

I had never seen so fine a man in my life before or since, and it seems to me that he had never appeared to me as beautiful as at that meeting in the editorial office when I sought his opinion of my work.

I remember another situation when he appeared so wonderfully fine. This occurred in the summer of 1914 at the Herzl memorial observance at the Baron de Hirsch Institute. Brainin spoke in Yiddish, an extraordinary outpouring of his soul. He was so deeply moved by his subject that for once he put aside his usual Germanized Yiddish and reverted to his native Mohilev Ruthenian dialect, free of Germanic terms and expressions.

(...) Clarence de Sola was the presiding officer of the solemn event. He was the acknowledged leader of the community for many decades; heir to his scholarly father, Abraham de Sola; descendant of the Josephs who came to Canada no later than Aaron Hart; Belgian consul; head of Canadian Zionism since before Herzl; architect of the third home of the Spanish and Portuguese Synagogue; interlocutor of Lord Balfour.

Clarence de Sola was listening to Brainin. This man of culture could — and probably did — appreciate the Jewish scholar who bore the cape of Germanic culture and the semantics of Hebrew phraseology. My eyes wandered to Clarence I. de Sola of Sephardi origin. He had known Herzl in his time, as de Sola was president of the Federation of Canadian Zionist Society for twenty-five years, and had attended Zionist congresses.

This cold, dry man kept looking at the orator like an amazed child overflowing with respect and wonder. He knew some German, but his Yiddish was weak.

It was not the Yiddish words that amazed him but the theme and the voice and the song that was pouring out from the heart. They captured him.

That evening — not always, for later de Sola turned on Brainin and persecuted him — he looked upon the speaker with awe as if he saw in him the incorporation of the inner and outer beauty that was Herzl.

Brainin was short, but I know this only by reason, and when I look at him in a group photo. Such a document aside, it is impossible to remember this. The impression that remains is of a tall man; it is impossible to describe or remember him otherwise.

The Jewish Institutions
of Montreal

Street scene in a Jewish neighbourhood, 1906.
Photo by W. Sharp, Montreal Standard.
Canadian Jewish Congress National Archives.

THE ENTIRE HISTORY of Montreal's Jewish community, as established by the new immigrants in the early twentieth century, may be found in the pages of the *Keneder Odler,* especially the most prosaic sections. The *Odler* was first and foremost an activist newspaper in the most literal sense — a publication that pleaded the case of the most disadvantaged, those in the community who were left out and were without resources. The situation of the poor was in itself a concern of the editors, but their special preoccupation was that these people should be served by organizations that would be sensitive to their culture and religious traditions, and that would promote the fundamental principle that it was up to the Jews of Montreal to mobilize to ensure the physical and moral welfare of all members of their community. Hence readers will find in these pages articles on the Baron de Hirsch Institute, on a fund-raising campaign for the Jews of Salonica, who had been the victims of a pogrom, and on typical charitable organizations such as those that visited the sick, clothed the poor, and cared for people with tuberculosis.

However, the *Odler* was not interested only in people in desperate situations or with incurable ills. The paper also pressed for the establishment of cultural institutions and schools to provide young people with a Jewish education, and it paid particular attention to the school question in Quebec. In many cases, the members of organizations that were still in their infancy rushed to the *Keneder Odler* to promote their points of view, to raise funds, or simply to persuade the Jews of Montreal to join their groups. More than once, the *Odler* lent its moral influence and its pages to these campaigns, in addition to publishing editorials at crucial points in the process. Montreal's Yiddish press made possible the founding of a certain number of institutions that were to play a key role in maintaining Jewish identity in the city, and in turn, these newly formed organizations provided the structure for a widespread readership without which the *Odler* would have been unable to survive for very long. Even *Der Veg,* which Brainin had envisioned as so different from the *Odler,* had taken the same path of militancy and community involvement, although at a more ideological and abstract level, as is shown by the final piece in this section.

The Institute and the People
Anonymous
Keneder Odler, March 17, 1909

Every bad thing has its share of good. This old rule was confirmed, for the thousandth time, most brilliantly at the Sunday night conference held at the Baron de Hirsch Institute.

It is of course sad when the Institute, the only established philanthropic institution in Canada, has not enough help for Montreal's poor Jewish population and should see itself on the verge of closing its doors. The bright side of this sad situation is that it reunited the Institute with the people.

For the Institute, the Montreal Jewish population was always divided in two very distinct parts: one part — several hundred members of the Institute which make contributions; and the second part — the majority of the population — which not only did not contribute, but only made use of the generosity of the first part.

The majority of the Jewish public was under the impression that all the millions left by the late Baron de Hirsch are in the Institute and therefore they do not have to contribute and can accuse with a clear conscience that the administration of the Institute gets rich using the poor.

The result was that, even when the Institute lacked money, and at our request presented a detailed report, no one wanted to negotiate with the *downtowners* and our report was not even opened. On the other hand, those in need could not imagine that the Institute lacked money and, in despair, started to raise scandals. Those who did not give or receive were watching impassively from a distance.

Of course this misunderstanding was detrimental only to the poor. It was generated by the lack of democratic spirit at the Institute. The Sunday Conference changed that. The Institute opened its doors not only for the dollars coming from the public at large, but also for its influence.

If the decisions reached at the Conference will be carried out, the Institute will become a popular institution in every sense of the word. The real winners will be the Institute and the poor. We believe that this will constitute one of the most important things to be accomplished in Montreal, with the help of the *Keneder Odler.*

Therefore, willingly or unwillingly, the administrators of the Institute took the first step. They opened both their doors and their books to everyone interested in philanthropic activity and willing to participate. Now the Institute can be controlled and influenced by the public, through their appointed representatives. The Institute is ready to be exposed to anyone's criticism, to listen to every opinion and to satisfy all legitimate claims. We have to carry out our duty, not towards the Institute, but towards the hundreds and hundreds of needy people.

We think that the twelve member committee will fulfil their tasks seriously and conscientiously. They will visit all the Jews from *downtown* and will invite them to become members of the Institute. We hope that this effort will not be for nothing.

In Montreal, there are certainly 500 Jews, non-members of the Institute, who can afford to pay five or ten dollars a year. They have not paid it so far. They should at least do it now. Their contribution could amount to 3-4,000 dollars. This is not a lot. It is about this amount the Institute distributes every month. This is something, though — such a sum could help several hundred hungry families for one month.

Some did not contribute to the Relief Fund of the Institute because they opposed it; others, from lack of compassion towards suffering fellows, while others only because they were not approached. From now on this has to change.

Now the enmity has to disappear, since its cause disappeared. The unresponsive ones should not remain indifferent, because the misery has reached the highest degree; and the twelve members will certainly do their job to approach potential donors.

The Baron de Hirsch Institute can and must remain a popular institution in the largest meaning of the word. (...)

On Fundraising in Montreal
Konrad Bercovici
Presumed to be in *Keneder Odler,* probably 1912

The unexpected report on the pogroms in Salonica came like thunder out of a blue sky.

Brainin decided this is no time for weeping. Writing will not alter the conditions of our kin. We must raise $1,000 and send it to the unfortunate.

Within a few minutes we raised $80 in the office of the *Odler*, from the lower and the several middle class people. When Brainin was about to thank one of the contributors, the man responded, 'Thank you for the opportunity to do my duty.'

The Baron de Hirsch Institute was conducting its annual elections and Brainin asked to speak; he urged immediate aid for the victims. As I listened I was certain that the thousand dollars would be raised there and then. All the wealthy citizens of the community were there. The sum total was $180, and this largely because of the energy of the former president Lyon Cohen.

From there we went to the Young Men's Zionist Literary Society where Brainin was to deliver a scholarly address. Instead he made his appeal. Within a few minutes they collected $30.

We left for the Russian-Polish Sick Benefit Society. Wolofsky understood the situation. Brainin's address resounded like the funeral march of Chopin on the demise of a nation, a march which would revive it and teach it the art of arms when necessary. Those present immediately contributed $50.

We arrived at the Hebrew Sick Benefit Society after their meeting, but their officers had done our work for us. They pledged $50 and Brainin had but to thank them.

We stopped in at the King George Society. Brainin sounded as an echo of the martyrs, and those who had remained to hear him raised over $20 within minutes. In the meantime the society delivered another $25 to the *Odler* for the cause.

We arrived at the Montreal Hebrew Association after their meeting; only four members had remained, but the chairman took it upon himself to pledge $10 in the meantime. We came too late also to the assembly of the Shoemakers Protective Society. When the last three members at the door had emptied their pockets, the contribution was $2.25.

We went home after midnight tired and broken. In the morning we received an envelope with $9. The pulse was beating hard.

We Must Found a *Bikur Kholim* in Montreal
Reuben Brainin
Keneder Odler, June 18, 1914

On various occasions we have already published letters saying that in Montreal we are lacking a *bikur kholim* organization such as exists in almost all other cities in the world where there is a Jewish population.

From time to time we have visits from long time residents, or from newcomers who have lain in local hospitals without visitors to say a friendly word.

Particularly sad is the situation of Jewish women who know no English, and have no relatives or acquaintances here. When they suddenly find themselves hospitalized and they need to rely on their Christian neighbours in the absence of Jewish doctors, they have no one to talk with, and loneliness is the more painful. (...)

Christian patients are visited by their clergy who bring the consolation of their faith.

Jewish sick are not visited by rabbis, and pious Jews happen to pass away in hospitals without final rites, without seeing a Jewish face or hearing a fraternal word.

Yesterday our paper reported on the front page the complaints of Mr. Schneiderman, who told us of a *griner* in the General Hospital, following a serious operation, who was as alone as a stone. He had no relatives in Montreal, or *landslayt*, to visit him. He wept as he told an acquaintance, who had been at his side on the job and was his only visitor, that his loneliness was harder than his illness.

I ask: Is it possible that such reports will not touch our readers?

Is it possible that fraternal and sisterly feelings have vanished from the Jewish population of Montreal?

(...) That feelings of sympathy, mercy, have died out among our Jews, who are called 'merciful among the merciful'?

Our Talmud notes that a Jew with no sense of mercy is not descended from Abraham.

I wish to believe that Montreal Jews are no different from Jews in other cities; (...) that Jews continue to observe the commandment of visiting the sick, not to speak of universal humanity. (...)

A beginning must be made.

Jewish Poverty in Montreal
Reuben Brainin
Keneder Odler, February 21, 1913

The editorial offices of the *Odler* are visited daily by needy people with open or hidden problems and complications in their lives — men and women in need of help, advice, recommendations; women and men, young and old, in need of listeners and moral support. Jewish poverty and misery is often modest, abashed, shedding secret tears.

In the poorest Jewish homes they share their last pennies with canvassers for charity, their bread with neighbours who are hungry. In their society we still find cases of generosity, compassion, character, refinement and idealism. (...)

Probably more than elsewhere, Montreal Jews are generous and good hearted. Noble women devote energy to help the needy through the Hebrew Consumptive Aid Society, the *Hakhnoses-Orkhim,* the *Malbush Arumim,* the Hebrew Ladies Aid Societies, and others.

The needs of the Jewish population in Montreal are too great for these institutions to handle. They lack the means and strength to render the Jews independent and autonomous of assistance. (...) Only the least reserved of the poor, and the most unfortunate apply to the Baron de Hirsch Institute, especially since there is a certain prejudice in the community, an antipathy against this institution.

And because all available resources in Montreal Jewry are focused on the alleviation of material need, resources are lacking to help the spiritual need in Montreal. The Jewish Public Library, Talmud Torahs and the schools in Mile End and in Amherst Park lack resources to exist.

The Jewish School Issues in Quebec
A. Wohliner
Presumed to be in the *Keneder Odler,* 1912

They were too much the businessman to take risks. They were anglophone Jews for whom Judaism and Jewish pride were a (yellow badge) on their English backbone. They attempted to socialize with the others for fear that the "greenhorns" would make trouble. They had proceeded to Quebec to accept what would be given them and to kiss the hand that would give them nothing. They even blocked from view the fists of the Jews who were truly hurt.

Their argument was 'we cannot maintain our schools by ourselves. At the most we might have two schools, while Jewish children are scattered all over the city. Many Jewish children will need to attend Protestant schools in any case, and the Protestants will have a right to keep Jewish children from their schools.'

Two schools could have satisfied the major portion of the Jewish population at the time. Only the *Yahudim* who had already been accommodated in non-Jewish sectors, would have felt uncomfortable. (...)

Jews are too poor to maintain schools? This is sheer stupidity. When they raised moneys for the Young Men's Hebrew Association (YMHA) many Jewish names appeared on the honour roll. Jews own considerable real estate and pay substantial taxes to the Protestant board.

The city would certainly help the Jewish schools as it helps Protestant and Catholic schools. Jews would gain a measure of cultural autonomy, a measure of respect from the Protestants who now sneer at them, and a measure of sympathy from the French.

About the *Folksbibliotek*
Reuben Brainin
Keneder Odler, June 10, 1914

Through much effort, through the greatest strain, we have finally succeeded in opening the *Folksbibliotek* (People's library), in a suitable, good apartment of seven rooms, and to furnish the rooms, and to buy the newest (books), and to order all possible journals.

For more than a year we have been agitating in vain for help in the Montreal Jewish population, (...) there was not one Jew in all of Montreal to give a table, a chair, a book case for our *Folksbibliotek* and People's University. (...) Our young people desire books to read. The library is well attended on a daily basis.(...)

The program of the *Folksbibliotek* is to assemble all of Hebrew literature

— Bible, Talmud, Halakhic law, Jewish science, morality, Hassidism, all of Yiddish literature and literature in translation (...) all the works of Jewish genius.

The *Folksbibliotek* does not pursue particular political interests, but remains open to all classes and to satisfy the most varied intellectual needs of the Jewish population.

A number of young, and even older immigrants [are pursuing Jewish studies in a comfortable open atmosphere created by and for our people. We have prevented some young immigrants from falling into missionary traps. Others have avoided the undesirable vulgar leisure centres, the haunts of the ignorant.

Our collaborators have proven the need of a Jewish library to retain our élite.]

On the Task of *Der Veg*
Reuben Brainin
Presumed to be in *Der Veg* , January 1916

During these months I have learned that there are words in the press which confuse the mind, turn white into black, truth into lie and controversy. Printed words can poison, can render the air pestilential and ruin the public organism. I am convinced that the people need their own press where their needs and emotions are interpreted properly, where ritual murder accusations cannot be levelled against anyone just because he is disliked.

Der Veg appears in the most decisive, serious moment in world history and, particularly in Jewish history.

In this last great destruction our people, both deliberately and less consciously, seeks new means, ways and instruments to ensure their existence, in the immediate present and in the furthest future; not mere existence but an existence of worth that is justified nationally.

At this colossal moment the tragedy of the Jewish people has become clear to all thinking minds which can judge a tragedy at its most horrible apex.

Clearly, as a people, we cannot return to the old ways and forms of insecurity among the nations of the world.

To be or not to be? To reawake with a new force, or to die slowly? To emerge as winners from the Great Destruction, or to disappear shamefully without a trace? These are the questions before us.

Fortunately, to our distinct honour, the great Jewish masses, our intellectuals and our best and finest sons — all who are capable of life and are thirsty for life, all who are capable of battle and are ready for battle — have responded with a distinct yes, to reawaken and to win. The Great Destruction in the lands of war have evoked a renaissance in other lands of our dispersion.

The majority of our people is organizing for a vital objective; to demand at the coming tribunal of the nations our human and national rights in all lands, a demand that bears the stamp of Messianic days.

But simultaneously, the open and the concealed force of assimilation — hateful, backward and crippled — is also mobilizing, guiding its last energies to compromise and to betray our proud and independent movement of our masses and intellectuals.

It is at such a great moment of battle and of rebirth that *Der Veg* appears. Under the sign of new world history, into the dawn, we seek to rise for the Jewish people.

Der Veg takes its place with the refined and the courageous battlers who will awaken all constructive forces latent in all the corners of our suffering people, the entire last reserve of our hidden vitality.

In Canadian Jewry the word and the act must be honestly and courageously supported.

We are aware of the hard and responsible task *Der Veg* is assuming. Our birth pains have lasted nine months, for stumbling stones were constantly put in our way; we know who put them in place, and what the motives have been.

Strikes and Social Protest

Front page coverage of the children's strike (article, upper left) in the *Keneder Odler*, March 2, 1913. Over 500 students at Montreal's Aberdeen School went on strike to protest a teacher's anti-Semitic remarks.

IN THE EARLY DAYS of Montreal's Yiddish press, many members of the Jewish community already worked in the garment factories on St. Lawrence Boulevard or in related labour-intensive industries. The health conditions in these places were often appalling, the jobs were precarious and dependent on economic cycles, and above all, the workers had no collective power to affect their situation. Jewish revolutionary experience in Russia during the abortive insurrection of 1905, the high degree of organization of the community, and especially, the ability of Jewish workers in Montreal to stay abreast of major trends in the North American trade union movement would quickly lead to changes in the situation in the local sweatshops. In 1912 a general strike in the garment industry pitted several thousand mainly Jewish workers against bosses who were also Jewish. The owners whom the tailors and specialized workers confronted in the streets were often the very men who ran the major Jewish philanthropic organizations, the main synagogues, and the important fundraising campaigns in the city.

The *Keneder Odler* could not remain indifferent to such glaring social conflicts, especially since they had direct repercussions within the community. The paper very often took the part of the workers and low-wage earners in these struggles and always kept its readers informed of the latest developments, especially because, as Max Schneour reminded Reuben Brainin in 1912, most of its subscribers were themselves wage-earners and small business owners with modest incomes. However, neither the *Odler* nor *Der Veg* was a workers' publication in the strict sense, nor did they support the most radical socialist ideas. Other, more specialized Montreal Yiddish papers such as the *Folkstsaytung,* undertook to carry the flag of revolutionary ideas and to take principles such as class struggle and the dictatorship of the proletariat to their final conclusions. Hirsch Wolofsky, the owner of the *Odler,* was actually a partisan of capitalism with a social conscience and throughout his career held enlightened views on the exploitation of workers, but he himself always associated with the city's wealthiest Jews.

Three pieces in this section are about an episode in Montreal Jewish history that is little known today, but that had a great deal of impact at the time: a strike in the spring of 1913 by several hundred schoolchildren. The strike was provoked by the openly anti-Semitic comments of a teacher in an English Protestant school attended almost entirely by Jewish students. This incident shows that the most left-wing social protest techniques had penetrated the community's customs so deeply that even elementary school children knew how to organize and stand up against established authority and obtain immediate justice.

The Tailors' Strike
(unsigned news item)
Keneder Odler, August 30, 1907

THE TAILORS STRIKE
Justified Demands of the Workers.
That wages be paid weekly: The tailors seek
shorter hours and higher prices:
MANY CONTRACTS SETTLED

The tailors' strike begun several weeks ago created a bit of an impression in the Jewish community of Montreal. The unions are generally still quite weak here and the workers' courageous stand against the manufacturers and contractors has surprised all classes. Shop after shop declared strike. The sad condition of the workers brought them to despair and eventually they called for better wages and shorter hours.

In no city are shop conditions as sad as those in Montreal. Work is carried on in cellars and basements, places without light or fresh air. In addition, workers slave from early to late at night, and when the time comes to get paid, then they need wait for the good grace of the bosses. (...)

The Montreal branch of the United Garment Workers of America has been waiting for the contractors to unite with the workers against the manufacturers because of certain common interests. But the contractors thought otherwise, and nothing came of the deal.

The workers are courageous and feel that their victory is close. Manufacturers are surrendering one after another, and only the stubborn are persisting.

Local 134 of the Tailors meets every Tuesday in the Labour Temple. The pressers meet Saturday evenings, and the waist, Local 116, on Monday evenings. Mr. Miller has also organized a ladies' union. They meet at the same place. A charter has been sent for them.

The following manufacturers and contractors have settled on union conditions: Montreal Waterproof Company, Vineberg and Company, H. Kellert and Sons, and some workers with Freedman Brothers.

Strikes continue at Chaim Gotlib, Feldstein and Siegel, Cohen and Levinson, and Standard Clothing Company. (...)

Daughter of the Jewish People
Letter to Editor
Keneder Odler, December 27, 1912

In Russia I was a devoted revolutionary, with my whole heart and soul, nourishing the dream of liberty, living for the salvation of the Russian nation. But we sacrificed even more for the Jewish nation. Many of my colleagues also believed that they would be liberated together with the fall of tyranny and slavery; the Jews, too, would develop culturally. It was a beautiful time of sacred hopes, of sacred ideals, of enthusiastic battle. There I felt I was searching for the Jewess and the human being (in myself) with full awareness.

That happy time is past. Fate, need, circumstance has cast me on to the shores of Canada, into a Montreal shop. What a change it has been for me in the seven years I have been in cold Canada! My identity has died within me. I am no longer the fine Jewess and the revolutionary fighter I had been. Difficult, sad, boring shop work and the petty concerns of shop life are mine. The Jewish woman that I have become in Canada finds no spiritual nourishment, and when the Jewess in our women becomes weakened, the human being in us becomes colourless and powerless.

I seem to remember that you once wrote, 'The new Judaism is waiting for the new Jew and, above all, for the new Jewess.' But where will she come from? Who cares for the Jewish daughters? Who lectures to us specifically? Which of the Jewish literary spokesmen address themselves to us and seek to strengthen our Jewish awareness?

An Open Letter to Reuben Brainin
Max Schneour
Keneder Odler, July 17, 1912

Worthy sir!

It was with great joy that I heard last winter the news that happy chance has brought you here to become editor of the *Keneder Odler*, (...) a joy for the entire Jewish population of Montreal to find Reuben Brainin in our midst, at the head of the local Jewish press. You were received with enthusiasm everywhere, and still now wherever you appear in public you are welcomed; especially by the working population in Montreal, which is the majority of the readers of the *Keneder Odler*.

The joy of the working population was twice as great, first to have a real paper to read and, secondly, it was certain that, in the event that a powerful word will be needed in its defence, Mr. Brainin, it will come from you. And now to my point.

There has been a tailors' strike in effect already for some six weeks, with four thousand courageous heroes lined against a few bosses, 4000 men fighting with their lives for their rights — for the right to have more leisure to enjoy life.

Since you are in Montreal, this is the first such phenomenon, Mr. Brainin, and what are you doing for the strikers, where are your editorials which should burn to defend the Jewish workers? Where are your ideals, your spirit for the fight for freedom, your ideal of equality and justice, that which you preach so often?

I am no striker, and my personal life is not affected. Only in observing the heroic battle of the brave working women and men, I am surprised at your attitude towards all these heroes. We do not hear a word from you. You might as well be a thousand miles from the battlefield.

You have once (not in one, but three articles) quoted the Talmud in defence of ethical values. I will, of course, not criticise your writing. But your present indifference is a surprise to me, indeed a riddle. How can you not react, the champion of all that is noble and free, how can you be so silent in the issue? When you and only you should be attacking the bosses? I remember my student days in Germany when you (...) learned that the relationships between Russian Jewish students in Berlin were not sufficiently moral. I remember that the pamphlets you wrote served as knouts to condemn them, I remember how we nationalist students would listen to your precious words. I cannot allow your coldness to the strike, no matter under what pressure. I am more than certain that men such as you do not sell their ideals for a mess of potage, and therefore show my surprise.

You expressed in private that your sympathy is with the strikers. Naturally, how can it be otherwise? But from you, Mr. Brainin, we expect more than sympathy. You probably remember the story of the wealthy innkeeper in his warm room, full of sympathy for a poor man in the cold weather begging shelter, who spoke of the freezing man outside. (...)

Strike of Yiddish School Children in Aberdeen School
Reuben Brainin
Keneder Odler, March 2, 1913

A strike of school children in Montreal is the latest sensation.

This time it is Jewish pupils on strike after a teacher insulted the pride of the Jews. (...) The Jewish students of Aberdeen School on St. Denis Street went on strike because, according to their explanations, a teacher of grade six, Miss McKinley, had insulted the feelings of the Jewish students by saying that Jews are dirty.

According to them: She said that when she first came to the school as a student it had been very clean, but since the Jewish children arrived the school had become dirty. She is also reported to have said that she would bring to the committee that Jewish children should be shut out of Aberdeen school.

On Thursday five students, Harry Singer, Frank Sherman, Joe Orenstein, Moses Skibelsky and Moses Margolis, had a meeting and decided to call a general strike unless the teacher apologized. When the expected apology of the teacher did not come, the students refused to further frequent the school.

The following day the children returned to school in the morning to pick up their text books and scribblers, but the teacher locked the door to them. The pupils sent younger children to each class with the call for a general strike. Soon 500 responded and some were named for picketing duty, as is the custom in all strikes.

The young strikers marched through the streets to the offices of the *Odler* where a spokesman for the newspaper promised them all possible support. They then marched to the Baron de Hirsch Institute.

A representative from the *Odler* called on the school principal Mr. Caulfield, but the latter refused to issue a statement, referring the matter to the Board of Education.

The Legislative Committee of the Baron de Hirsch Institute met in the office of S.W. Jacobs. (...) A committee consisting of Rabbi H. Abramowitz and Mr. Jacobs was appointed to deal with the matter. They met with the principal. The teacher expressed her regret for having made inappropriate comments. She said, though, that she was misunderstood by the children.

Rabbi H. Abramowitz and Mr. Jacobs requested that without exception the children be accepted back by the school and that the teacher be transferred to another class. The matter was left in the hands of the School Commission, and the Board of Education will determine this.

The Legislative Committee of the Baron de Hirsch Institute recommended that the children return to school while the Jewish committee negotiated with the commissioners. (...)

When Rabbi Abramowitz and Mr. Jacobs drove to the school the strikers greeted them with resounding screams, and when the committee left the school the striking students received them with shouts of 'Hurrah.'

This Monday all the students should come to the school and the Baron de Hirsch Legislative Committee will see to it that their grievances are remedied.

Strike of Yiddish School Children
Reuben Brainin
Presumed to be in the *Keneder Odler,* March 1913

The incident in the School which evoked a pupil strike after a teacher offended the Jewish people is a major contribution to Jewish renaissance.

Christian society let it pass as a minor event; the Jewish public took it as child's play. Some Jews considered it unfortunate. Why arouse the geese? But the inquiring eye will see that there is much to learn in the case.

This without entering into the justice of the case or whether children should resort to strikes. The first to protest should be the parents, and it is the parents who should demand rights and justice for them. But what interests me is that the children did not seek justice for themselves; it was their national sensibility that was offended and that provoked their little fists against their highest government (for to children their teachers and schools are the highest government).

We need to think much about this first sprouting of a generation which is new in our exile history, a free generation which is discarding the chains of diaspora, which no longer bends its head, no longer begs for justice but takes what is not accorded it freely.

The New Generation
Reuben Brainin
Keneder Odler, March 4, 1913

(...)

All this lies hidden in the children's strike. The tender soul of the Jewish child would not dare strike for such a matter against a teacher if the threads of national rebirth were not weaving in their souls. And their parents have a lot to learn from them.

In ancient times the gates of education were locked to Jews and children were the first to feel exile. When they first came into the world, they were locked into the *kheder* and the *beys hamidrash* where they neither knew nor felt the taste of *galut.*

But since schools were opened to Jews, the Jewish child began to feel *galut.* Every skulking teacher or professor had the right to insult and stifle the Jewish soul of a child. He always protested, but his exilic parents always suppressed all that is Jewish in the child to the point of denial of his self. But a new air has entered the Jewish situation. Self denial has has been transformed into proud self-assertion. The *galut* type is beginning to disappear and the Jew is already beginning to feel like a human being, a human being who has as much right to be born as all people.

And who has brought out this new Jewish spirit? The best children of the preceding generation. The select few of the last fifty years have come to feel the rottenness that has entered the Jewish soul (...) (and) have begun through the creation of a new Jewish culture to raise the flag of national rebirth. If we hear of echoes of a Yiddish word in the distant corners of America, if we see new books on the market, if we see big daily and weekly journals in Hebrew and Yiddish, if we observe a new atmosphere in the movement of Jewish life, we have only them to thank.

And if we find in Montreal a miniature Jewish world of 600 small soldiers marching hand in hand in defence of Jewish honour and in pride, out of respect for their people, let no one believe that this stems from North American liberty. (...) It derives from the literary evenings in Jewish institutions, it is the product of Hebrew readings and presentations which young people hear and absorb. (...)

The act of these children is an honour unto us. Many Christians will learn the new Jewish sense of honour.

Strikers in Montreal
Reuben Brainin
Presumed to be in the *Keneder Odler*, January 1914

Monday evening I witnessed a fearful scene, so terrible that I have lost my rest ever since. The picture does not fade from my eyes. I cannot be silent. The Jewish community must take measures that this shall never be repeated.

I was in my office at six in the evening when the telephone began ringing to tell me that a pogrom Kishinev-style was going on outside Vineberg's.

I proceeded at once with J.B. Miller to the scene of the violence. As I got off the sleigh I was roughly seized by three policemen as if I were a condemned criminal. Mr. Miller informed the police sergeant, who happened to be his friend, that I was editor of the *Odler*, and they released me.

It was clear that the strikers conducted themselves peacefully from beginning to end; no outcries, no provocation, no unrest from their side. But the police were brutal to all peaceable passers-by opposite the Vineberg shop, using fists and clubs, beating out wildly at the people passing. Jewish men and women were struck and had bones broken without the slightest provocation. I had never witnessed such wild police brutality in my life.

There are labor demonstrations in the large centres of Europe; as long as workers and strikers are peaceful, the police stay in hidden corners and do not touch anyone with a finger. Even in Germany, where the police are strict and brutal, they never acted against peaceful demonstrations, even when hundreds of thousands marched on the streets.

Only in Russia, during the revolutions, or in Kishinev was anything like this ever seen.

Who is responsible for this police violence? Certainly not the workers and the citizens who were quietly marching on the street or returning home from work.

But whoever ordered the attack on peaceful citizens with clubs like wild Indians, the police had no right to carry out such an order.

Certainly the aldermen have a heavy duty to ascertain who were the guilty and to prevent such brutality in the future. Otherwise the citizenry is not secure in their lives, and the Jews who left Russia because they could no longer tolerate inhuman police brutality will have to taste Kishinev in free Canada.

Thank God law and justice reign in this country. We must demand security for our Jewish citizens. We must respond to the wildness of the police against peaceful Jewish citizens.

The Diaspora

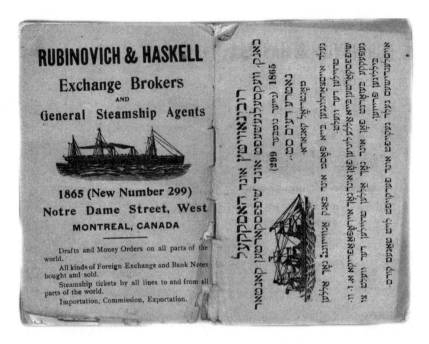

Pages from a Jewish almanac, 1905-1906, showing
advertisement for a shipping agent.
Dubitsky Collection, Canadian Jewish National Archives.

ONE OF THE MOST IMPORTANT roles of the Montreal Yiddish press was to disseminate firsthand information on Ashkenazi communities around the world on a daily basis. The Yiddish-speaking Jews of Canada at the time constituted only a minor branch of the great diaspora of Eastern European Jews, and there were still many personal emotional ties binding them to their region of origin, if not to the *shtetl* they had grown up in and only recently left. Anti-Semitic incidents such as the Beilis affair in 1913, pogroms like those that occurred in Kishinev in 1903 and again in 1905, and the outbreak of World War I, were of the greatest interest to the Jews of Montreal. They worried about the consequences of these events for their loved ones in the Old Country — sometimes a wife or children, most often a community that they had left behind only in body. As the memoirs of Medres and Wolofsky, two of the architects of the early *Keneder Odler,* amply demonstrate, the Montreal Jewish public reacted strongly to the persecution of their fellow Jews in the Russian Empire and in times of crisis snatched up any information available about them, including what was published in the local papers.

More broadly, the *Keneder Odler* paid attention to Jewish life all over the world, in democratic countries such as Great Britain, France, or Belgium and in societies that were much less liberal toward their minorities. The paper reported regularly on the level of tolerance shown to Jews in certain key cities such as Paris, St. Petersburg, or Rome, where the treatment of the Jews was a clear indication of the movement of European society as a whole with respect to anti-Semitism or civil liberties. The *Odler* sometimes even provided news of events concerning other minority communities that could have repercussions on how future Jewish immigrants to Canada might be greeted. This was the case, for example, of an article by Yehudah Kaufman on the arrival in June 1914, in the port of Vancouver, of the *Komagata Maru,* a ship holding several hundred Sikh immigrants which Canada drove from its territorial waters by military force.

The *Keneder Odler* also reported with great emotion on the tribulations of Sholom Aleichem in the last years of his life. The great Yiddish writer had fled Russia because of World War I and taken refuge in Denmark under very difficult conditions, and his renown was so great in the Yiddish-speaking world that his misfortunes aroused the sympathy of Jews in many countries, including Canada, and led them to raise funds for him.

On the Jews in London, England
Reuben Brainin
Presumed to be in the *Keneder Odler*, early April 1908

Now, (March 31, 1908) I have been here for eleven weeks studying the great book of London and its East End, chapter by chapter, line by line, letter by letter. Every detail interests me, every point in this notable book (...)

The Jews of the East End leave the impression of passengers at sea who have met with catastrophe; many have drowned; others were saved by good fortune on an island. They seem to be waiting for the happy accident of a ship that would take them elsewhere. Accident had brought them to an island, blind fate would carry them elsewhere. Life on the island is temporary. The more capable somehow earn a living, the others, unhappy, walk like shadows; they seize every opportunity of hope for minimum income. They are without skills. They do not like their occupations. Those in the trades do not know how to deal honestly with their customers. I wanted to know why so few Christians came to the East End stores or even to the Jewish areas of older established stores. I was told. 'This is not anti-Semitism, but the English are English, and even the poorest classes are accustomed to shop in well-swept stores, where the merchandise is orderly, the storekeepers are skilled in their trade and they are well served, where the purchases are neatly wrapped. The Jewish stores are in hopeless confusion.'

The Hebrew teachers and the religious clergy do not know their profession; they are in their function by chance. In this uncertain society of East European Jews there can be no flourishing of culture blossoms. Some hundred thousand Jews live in this uninteresting, vacant East End of London's ghetto. The more capable, healthier among them move slowly to America or to London's west or north, and the ghetto remains the home of the less skilled and the less capable, the less cultured, in the struggle for life.

The upper layer of intellectuals are distant, in every sense, from London, in an exile within an exile, with no contact with the Eastern Jews of London. It is a sad report, but one that leads us to thinking.

Polish and Romanian Jews in Belgium
Reuben Brainin
Keneder Odler, November 23, 1908

Among them are only a small number of wealthy ones — like Ignacy Bernstein, the author of *Yiddishe Shprikhverter* (Jewish Proverbs) — who live off their investments. They have chosen Brussels because it is the capital of a very free country, with many qualities desirable for those who would live in peace, in culture and in freedom. The Polish Jews are almost all poor; only few have achieved anything.

Polish Jews have no contact with Belgian Jews except that the very poor received some support from the latter. The Belgian Jews look down upon the Poles (...) the Belgian Jews, in particular the wealthy ones, have false, distorted notions of the Polish Jews.

Among the newly immigrated from Russian Poland are a few small scale carton manufacturers, some keepers of small stores. The rest work in various factories or are tailors, carpenters, glove makers, leather workers and salesmen. Women and girls among the Polish immigrants (a few are Lithuanians) are dressmakers, work at jackets, scarves, gloves, and in some large fashion shops. It is to be noted that the biggest style shops in Brussels (A. Hirsch and Mitz) are in Jewish hands. Wages are no higher than in Warsaw or Lodz.

In Belgium, immigrants must learn two languages, French and Flemish, in order to exist or to reach a higher position. All of them study French more assiduously, even though Flemish is much easier to learn for those who know Yiddish. The Jew does not know what the morrow will bring; he believes instinctively that French, the universal tongue, will be more useful to him in the future than Flemish which is limited to Belgium.

I have visited some working families in their homes to see how they live. I have met gentle and very refined people among them. Some had studied in *yeshivot* (and are still attached to all that is printed in the dotted alphabet.). I have met some workers who receive *Unser Lebn* from Warsaw, and the most recent Yiddish literature. Others receive Hebrew books. In all of Brussels there is not a single Jewish bookstore. You cannot even secure a Bible or a prayer book here. Purchasers have to turn to Antwerp (where "Cohen and Colt" have set up a decent Jewish bookstore), or directly to Warsaw. In all Brussels there is not one Jewish library or reading room where one can get something Yiddish or Hebrew. The more intelligent workers from Warsaw have complained that there is no centre of discussion for those interested in letters, so that it is no wonder that a part of the Jewish youth has become corrupted by the merry and light social life of Brussels; are swallowed by the alien society and estranged from Judaism and from family life. They make no real contact with Belgian society among whom, even among Belgian workers, there are not a few who utilize their leisure for self-education.

On Sunday I visited a capmaker, a *maskil,* at his small two-room apartment. His neighbours with their wives and small children (craftsmen from Warsaw and Lodz who had arrived a year or two ago) came in the evening as guests, and one of them read from the new Yiddish literature. They asked me endless questions about the Czernowitz conference on languages and about the new freethinkers ditto for Czernowitz.

To my question of their experience with Russian students new in Belgium, "(...) They are a disgrace to us and they are not interested in us, nor have they any sense of idealism."

I was not in Brussels long enough to confirm the accuracy of their statements.

The newly immigrated established a new community by the name of the Guardians of the Faith. The custom of the Orthodox community is according to the German rite in Poland. Their rabbi, Dr. Bamberger, a German, is beloved by the Russian and Polish Jews. Its 120 members have established a Welcoming of the Guests and a Ladies Aid Society.

On Sunday evening I again visited the Belgian "Maison du Peuple," founded by Social Democrats, where Russian Jewish students and workers of different nationalities eat, drink, hear lectures on various subjects, and attend theatre. Characteristically the workers sit in their own sections: Belgians, Germans, Russian Jews each in their own corners at their own tables, (...) some speaking or attempting French. The air is smoke-filled, and many mothers even bring infants with them.

Saturday night, a Yiddish theatre troupe visited Brussels on their tour of the countryside. Tickets had been sold during the week to the Jewish workers for 'the world famous actor Berman and the prima donna Mme. Merban in the comedy *Orphan Chassya.*' I arrived on time, at 8:30 but the curtain did not rise till 10:00. (...) (I had been told that in the past, companies had sold tickets and fled with their 'take' without performing). [There were not more than twenty in the audience (...) in a small room in an inn; the audience applauded the actors and the orphans and commented as the children played loudly. I wonder whether the cast was able to return to Antwerp fifty miles away.]

Some time ago a Zionist group had been formed, but the sponsoring officers left the city [and Brussels' Zionism is showing no life, contrary to the Antwerp situation.]

The Jews in France
Reuben Brainin
Presumed to be in the *Keneder Odler,* February 1909

In recent years French Jewry has sunk to a lower level, its Judaism has become a peel, devoid of name or content.

Several causes led to this catastrophe. The Dreyfus case led the petty merchant souls of French Jewry to fear anti-Semitism, persecutions and false accusations; they avoid the French and fear radicals as the mortal enemy.

There are probably more profound, psychic, historical and racially instinctive reasons why the Jews of France, who have severed the strong and fine threads that bind them to Judaism, have not been baptized.

One element is the separation of church and state and the fact that the present government is liberated in matters of faith. French Jews conceive of Judaism only as a religion, not as a national reality. They sense instinctively that the black clericalism can bring them only troubles and persecution, possibly pogroms à la russe, consequences of the black poisonous hatred which is appearing in the corners of a nation which had never been close to Judaism. These Jews suppress and hide increasingly all signs of Jewishness and of tradition which remained in their midst. They accept the ostrich policy which believes that if they bury their eyes in the sand, if they will not openly see the enemy and that foe will not see them.

Conversion is not the French style and, of course, style is the queen of French social life. Her Majesty la Mode forbids conversion and ridicules it.

So most of intellectual French Jewry entered the ranks of *libre pensée* and freemasonry and are more distant from Judaism than even a few years ago. When a Western European Jew discards religion he tears all bonds which unite him with his brethren and alienates himself from Jews.

Significantly, the late Rabbi Zadok Cohen was one of the greatest Jews of his time. I had known him for twelve years, and my admiration of his great Jewish soul grew with time as of a wise man concerned with all developments in Judaism, who was in constant contact with the great men of Israel. He responded to every appeal; he utilized his influence on wealthy French Jews and led Baron Edmond de Rothschild into the Hovevei Zion. Himself no minor Hebrew stylist, he followed current literature and science. A perpetual gentleman, he conversed with Anatole France and Rabbi Samuel Mohlever.

His successor as chief rabbi, Alfred Levy, is the contrary to Rabbi Zadok Cohen. Like most Paris Jews, the Rothschilds opposed his appointment and supported the candidacy of Rabbi Cohen's son-in-law, Prof. Israel Levy. But the Jews in the province disliked his relationship with the alien Russian Jews.

The present chief rabbi is a nullity, without learning, Torah wisdom, or deeds, very distant from Judaism, deliberately ignorant of Jewish affairs; a reasonably adequate speaker but devoid of content. Jewry had never heard of him. When a prominent Zionist quite properly slapped his face in public, the community in Lyon said that the event resounded throughout the Jewish world. Nearly seventy years old he has never published an article or achieved a single act on behalf of Jews or Judaism.

Among Brethren
Reuben Brainin
Keneder Odler, January 9, 1910 (?)

[In Russia] the psychology of it is that the more educated classes, who had already experienced assimilation, and had already been through the entire process of being like their Christian neighbours, are now returning to their Jewish self-esteem, and protest against their former assimilating tendencies, whilst the less educated, who have not as yet gone through the process, have not yet become as nationalistic. It is interesting to note that even the converted Jews have joined in this campaign and are averse to speaking Russian; we often hear one telling the other to speak *mamme loshen.*

In St. Petersburg, there is a Society for the Advancement of Hebrew, of which the very highest Jews of the city are members and in which they have taken an active and lively interest. This society is ahead of any other Jewish organization of a like nature, and the only medium of conversation within its walls is Hebrew. When I was in that city recently, I delivered a lecture before that body in Hebrew, and in conversing with them I was pleasantly surprised to see such a large number of Jews all of whom speak our ancient tongue so fluently. This Yiddish movement I have just referred to is purely a stepping stone to the use of this language. Wherever and whenever possible they lose no opportunity of introducing Hebrew words into the jargon. In Galicia, the cultivation of the Hebrew language stands on an exceptionally high level, and is spoken and read by the highest and lowest, male and female, student and workman alike.

It is humorous to see and hear Jewish workmen on a church steeple putting up a cross and singing Hebrew melodies.

In the universities the Jewish students until recently registered as Polish speaking; now they place themselves on the rolls as Hebrew speaking. In the largest Jewish business houses, banks, factories, etc., all the correspondence, books, telegrams, and so forth, are carried out in Hebrew. Since the Russian revolution there has been a marked revival of the study of the Hebrew language.

Yiddish as a language has no future at all, because it is being forgotten and ignored by the rising generation. For that reason alone Hebrew must be cultivated and propagated amongst us, and must be recognized as our living language. For, if this be not done, the Jews will have two dead languages — Yiddish and Hebrew. We must have one common language, Hebrew, to unite us, even when we are scattered amongst other nations of the world.

In Germany, at present there is a new development amongst the better class families. These are anxious for their children to receive a thorough Hebrew education, and even go to the extent of engaging Jewesses with a thorough knowledge of the Hebrew language as governesses. The Society for Hebrew Culture in Berlin, of which I have the honour to be president, and which is composed of students at the universities, until recently had ninety-five percent Russian Jewish students who had come to study in Berlin. Today it is the reverse, ninety-nine percent of its members are German Jews. Such a stronghold has Hebrew become amongst our people in Germany.

In Palestine, and all the oriental countries, Hebrew has always been, more or less, a living language; but of recent years there has been a marked further renaissance. Since the Young Turk movement has started, there has also been the 'Young Jew' movement, in a sense that the rising generation has taken up the revival of the Hebrew language and the Hebrew culture. The Spanish and the Portuguese Jews are now cultivating the language, are speaking it, and are teaching it most energetically to their children. In the schools, Hebrew is the medium of instruction, for both Jew and Arab. Even the servants who came out with some of the Russian emigrants speak nothing but Hebrew, for the very good reason that in many localities they could not be understood in any other language. The instances I relate must convince the most pessimistic and lethargic Jew.

I paid a visit to the Talmud Torah in the Baron de Hirsch Institute, under the Rev. Levin, and I found the children all enthusiastic and eager to learn. I asked them questions in Hebrew, and they answered them in the same tongue. They, naturally, have a great deal to learn yet, but it is a beginning; the spirit is there and they stand in the right way of acquiring a good knowledge of the language.

I am greatly optimistic. The Judaism I see is neither strictly reform nor entirely orthodox. I see the *via media*. Those of the ultra reform element, who shall not become entirely assimilated, or indifferent, will become more conservative; but orthodoxy will also have to approach nearer the middle way. There will of course, always be parties in Judaism, all in accordance with the countries where we dwell, but there has been a distinct revival all over the world.

The Power of Darkness
A.M. Mandelbaum
Keneder Odler, June 16, 1914

[In San Francisco at the brilliant maritime exposition of 1915 the long rows of Christian maritime power will show the power of pure Christian nations, the refinements of swords and uniform, and demonstrate their greatness and strength. And Italy sends a Jew as its representative![1]] It seems that in doing so Italy will be desecrating the Christian festival. Good men with Christian hearts and pure Christian souls will faint at the sight as they will think of the poor, long mustachio-decorated, wandering Victor Emanuel and his long-alleged possible connection with Jews. Others will trouble to prove documentarily the King's origin in Jewish seed, God forbid. After all, we are dealing with priest's people who are nearer to the heavens than to sinful earth (...)

One way or another we must credit the priests for doing their duty. This time they have confirmed their true black colours. It could simply not have been otherwise.

Will the Exposition suffer from this *kherem*?

In no sense.

If the Panama Exposition will not have its proper éclat, if many European firms will not display their collections in San Francisco, it will be for other reasons. The success or failure of the world exhibition does not depend on the grace of a score of clergymen or several "sacred" relics.

If the convention of the Catholic priests withdraws its sessions from San

Francisco in 1915, only a few hotels and coffee houses, where the sacred holy men would satisfy their material needs, would suffer.

The priests cannot have the slightest influence on the exposition as a whole. It is hard to tell whether the Catholic manufacturers in all America will listen to the curious *kherem*. True, faith is quite a fine thing, but business is business.

The polish of the cross will never compete with the cling of the coin.(...)

If the Panama Exposition would depend entirely on several dozen Catholic priests, they would do well to dismantle all the little structures on the field and revoke the show.(...)

As the Catholic boycott is being conducted because of "our" (Ernesto) Nathan who represents Christian Italy, we the Jews cannot ignore this hostile attack.

We cannot permit that our assimilated *(fargoyeshtert)* Nathan should alone represent his race at the World Exhibition. Nathan has come to America with a pure Italian passport. He has been welcomed with bugles and trumpets in our harbour by "his" Christian Italians.

Rightly or wrongly we did not welcome "our" Nathan. Rightly or wrongly we left this "job" for those to whom he came in fact. Jews have a sharp sense of smell. Jews could not and dared not bring forward their letters of welcome to a *Señor* who had not come to them. If Jews ought to protest sharply against the clerical excommunication it is not because of the half-Jewish *Señor* Nathan, but rather for the honour of the Jewish name.

Jews should be represented at the Christian World Exposition not as Italians but as Jews. Jews should erect their own structure and raise their blue-white flag at the mast.

Not by dark *kherem* would we direct our attention to the dark forces.

The Jews of the entire world must build on the shivering waters of the Pacific their own national prestigious building, a minor temple of Jewish art *(beys hamigdash)*, for the display of the spiritual treasures, of the national values of the Jewish people,(...) where our values will be determined in appreciation of their lines and characteristics.

As the evil forces come to see that we can produce not only (...) mayors for sacred Rome but Jewish geniuses and *geonim* in whose hearts are impressed the Jewish, the mysterious name *(shem hameforash)*[2] and who bear lofty and proudly the genealogy of their descent.

Jews should, and must, show the black cowled subjects of the black family that they do not believe in the instruments of *kherem*, that they can use against darkness in far more appropriate, more pacific and more humane, and at the same time, sharper instruments.

A Jewish building on the shores of the Pacific in 1915 will be the most effective response to the clerical excommunication, pronounced against the Jewish representative of Christian Italy.(...)

Nathan's origin will soon be cloaked among the national structures in the Exposition field.(...)

---

[1] First sentence is somehat paraphrased
[2] Hasidic reference

The Problem of the Sikhs
Yehudah Kaufman
Keneder Odler, June 4, 1914

Here stand the seven to eight hundred Sikhs from the shore like lepers locked out of the land where they placed their last hopes, still standing and awaiting the response of the Canadian people, more correctly, the Canadian Senate. This question could be fatal not only to them but also to tens of thousands of their brethren.

For the seven to eight hundred determined emigrants are the precursors of a great movement that must repeat in world history. They are a great deputation of the nation of hundreds of millions sent by the profoundest and poorest of the peoples of the Far East, addressing to the civilized world with the most heart rending petition.

(...) Countless thousands of years and generations our parents have been fighting in our own land against the rich and wild nature which has refused to feed them. Millions of people fell like flies, dying of the most shameful death known to mankind: hunger. It has discouraged many of our elders, creating indifference to life, and turning them into living corpses. But most of our people have not surrendered the fight, being spiritually rich enough to give the world a Buddha. They had the courage to believe in life regardless of the black death which dominates our land. Courageously they fought with all their power to tear from the earth (...) the bites of bread. (...) But all in vain; hunger and death are all that face them.

Economically exhausted, politically weak, we the children of the ancient cultured nation have determined on the most frightening course in the history of our nation. Some of us have determined to revolt and share the fortune beyond the greatest ocean, far from their motherland, and must seek bread for their brethren who remain on the ancient historical land. (...)

Now we stand at your threshold and await your response, younger brother nations, (...) [Australia and Canada].

"The future which they wish to help build is based not only on their ancient historical past.(...) They come not only as to strangers: recognizing once and for all their political subservience under Britain, they come as British subjects to British lands, remaining ever faithful to the interests of the ocean-dominating kingdom.

But the ears of those to whom the justified petition of demands is directed remain deaf. The ports and gates remain silent and locked, as the waves of the sea which whisper about the brand new India question. The waves are sad as they carry the new wandering nation from land to land, from door to door, ever meeting the same fate.

Now the seven to eight hundred stand in Canadian waters, as they think and wonder: a land so rich, and extensive as the entire world and bears under two percent of the population of India; a land requiring willing power, whose most important obligation is work — how can such a land in justice not accept them with open arms?

The bitter truth responds from the shores with rejection. 'Why' they ask the waves, and receive no answer: The echoes sound back to us, 'Why?' But who on the shore hears?

Article by Sholom Aleichem
Keneder Odler, August 1914 (?)

I write you briefly about the catastrophe which has happened to our brothers, especially the Russians in the German spas who have been taken captive. Some have simply been driven out of Germany and barely made it to Copenhagen.

My family are among those who have lost everything but the shirts on our backs, but have made it to the noble cultured little land, Denmark. We cannot return to Switzerland; and certainly not to Russia. The few Russian rubles I have are worthless. I have no notion what will happen to us. My only hope is that ships will sail for the U.S. But I do not have enough for ten steamer tickets. Our only comfort is that we are not alone. Many of our people are imprisoned in Berlin, in Stettin, in Kiel; others are sent for war work.

Bialik, Schneour, Cohen are among the imprisoned. They say Sokolow is in Berlin, free. Dr. Chlenov sailed for Stockholm as doctor. Life in Russia is disrupted; no Jewish papers.

Yesterday's rich men, today's paupers are at loose ends. (...)

I participate in a concert here for the refugees. I hope they never have to make one on behalf of my own family. May God have mercy. If Germany is defeated, it will be by the work of the Jewish god.

I was with the Russian minister sharing our misfortune aboard the small Swedish vessel on which we barely escaped.

Please have this letter printed in the Jewish papers, and advise, whence shall come my help?

A Letter From Sholom Aleichem
Sholom Aleichem
Keneder Odler, October 18, 1914

(To the publisher of *Di Tsayt* in London)
Copenhagen, 22nd September.

Dear Friend Morris Meyer!

Of all things, I am writing you from bed. I have become sick from all my troubles and it seems to me quite seriously, if not too seriously. It seems I will not escape from the hands of the angel of death quite scot free.

This means, I think, that I am saying farewell to the world. *Oy vey,* in such a time to die? The act of a fool, but what can I do? I am hatefully trapped. That Germany decided to capture the entire world, am I at fault? Ha-ha. As one who is thinking of the world to come chats with professors about operations, (and feels in his heart that the end is not far away), I want to be a fool and make a prophecy.

Whether the Germans will conquer the entire world or not, a (...) new world is coming. New horizons are already appearing. Empires will be destroyed. Little nations will be built. Nations will be constructed; peoples will be torn apart; among all peoples, our Jewish people Israel will be privileged with its own new times, sort of Messianic times. They will experience much consolation *Nachmu, Nachmu, Ami* (be comforted, be consoled, my people); our little prophets will sing. The Zionists will sing their song. And where will I then be?

(...) If this reaches you, have it printed and send me the page here and a copy to Switzerland. The world catastrophe will end one day. Let the children read it, if I will no longer be. And if I am still here, so much the better. Truthfully, the world will lose nothing with my passing. But I will lose so much! I will not be here just when the Messiah, the long awaited Messiah, the real Jewish freedoms will be arriving. My eyes will not see the liberated, reconciled Jew. Well, at least my children should live to see it!

Another matter pains me, I have not completed my autobiography, and I probably will not complete it, even though I write bit by bit about these times of confusion and about the world war also, as you requested, and I will send them to you page by page, piece by piece. Print them. They cannot be sent home to Russia. It is also hard to send them to America. So you print them. But do not fail to send me the issues of your paper. It is long since I have seen a Jewish word (and send me clippings of my articles). I am at least comforted by having my entire family with me here. And do you know, my friend, the nature of my sickness? I am dying for a drink of water. The sea is too small. So thank God, I am provided that, even in a strange land burdened by a considerable family, without means of support (for at home I am totally ruined), I shall not starve to death but will die of thirst!

Thank God for this favour! At least they shall not say: Sholom Aleichem starved to death. *Feh*! Thirst is more refined. Original. Many Jews starve to death but only Sholom Aleichem died of thirst. Quite a man!

Last week we had an evening in aid of the Jewish war refugees, naturally with my participation. All the Jews of Denmark came! All the workers —and we raised some money too. And now they are setting up a kitchen for the poor. I read my work, naturally the audience laughed. But it did not occur to anyone there that the poorest and the least fortunate immigrant was I!

I will write you per your request from time to time. Let your paper be the only one through which I can chat with my beloved Jews. America is shut off; Russia is darkness and mist. At least may a few words remain with you as a memorial from your friend, the eternal wanderer,

Sholom Aleichem.

The Canadian Jewish Congress

R. Brainin (first row far left), Lyon Cohen (first president of the Canadian Jewish
Congress), H.M. Caiserman (General Secretary of the CJC), and H. Wolofsky
(with moustache) and other delegates attending the Canadian Jewish Congress
founding Plenary Assembly at the Baron de Hirsch Institute
on Bleury Avenue, 1919.
Canadian Jewish Congress National Archives.

ONE OF THE GREAT DEBATES within the Canadian Jewish community in this period concerned the creation of an umbrella organization that would bring together all the Jews of the country. The idea itself was not new, because at various times in their history, the Jews of Montreal had institutions that were well enough established to claim to represent all residents of the city of the Hebrew faith, such as the Baron de Hirsch Institute, the Ladies' Hebrew Benevolent Society, or the Federation of Jewish Philanthropies. However, with the arrival of the Yiddish-speaking Jews came radical left-wing and Labour Zionist groups, trade unions dedicated to defending the workers, and even anarchist cooperatives that aggressively espoused atheism. This led to rifts in the organizational fabric of the community, destroying the unanimity of the late nineteenth century and transforming the situation in Montreal.

All these new facets of the community did not integrate harmoniously with the middle-class, more ideologically cautious elements — given the language barrier and differences in sensibility that now separated large segments of the Montreal Jewish community. However, the outbreak of World War I in August 1914 led Canadian Jews to reconsider their reluctance to cooperate with one other. A few months later, the Russian government's persecution of Jews living near the front led a number of organizations in Montreal to spontaneously take up fundraising for the victims. The community quickly realized that these efforts would not be successful as long as the *downtowners* acted separately from the *uptowners* and the synagogues did not consult the garment industry unions. Moreover, Canadian Jews, who now wanted to press the Canadian and British governments to make their Russian ally listen to reason, had no one validated by democratic process to speak for the community.

The question was finally resolved in March 1919 when over 200 delegates from a variety of Jewish organizations throughout Canada met at the Monument National theatre in Montreal to found the Canadian Jewish Congress. This was the culmination of months, even years, of efforts by a group of mainly Yiddish-speaking activists determined to unite the Jews of the country. Unprecedented ferment surrounded this movement for institutional consolidation, which is evident in the tone and the issues raised in the articles in this section.

Reuben Brainin Calls for Foundation
of a Canadian Jewish Congress
Keneder Odler, 1915(?)

Great days have come for the Jewish people: days when our people suffer most bitterly and hope most stoutly; days when we are perhaps passing through the final, the most horrible chapter in the history of our exile, in which our ancient nation must fight like a young lion in its final and most important battle for liberation.

We have ourselves become great with these great days. Wherever the pulse of Jewish community life beats the Jewish masses are penetrated by an electric current, by one sentiment — the sense of responsibility for the great historic moment.

In an instant the young American Jewish community has sensed the historic role that it must assume in Jewish life. From within them has arisen deep, broad and far-reaching popular movements; all across American Jewry there comes the call for the organization and for unity.

The Jewish Congress has become the slogan of the Jewish society — a Congress to be convened by the people itself, where those chosen will express the iron will of the people to struggle for its freedom. At this Congress there shall be heard the cry of a people long robbed of its human rights. At this Congress the nation will declare openly to the entire world that, in spite of all persecutions and humiliations of centuries and of millennia, it has not ceased to exist as a people and still believes in its right to such an existence. At this Congress we shall clearly and specifically state what we wish and what we expect from the Great Powers at the moment when the fate of nations is being determined for centuries to come.

A Congress of all the Jews of America has become the slogan of courage for us. To it we bind our best hopes for a better future for our people and for a better Jewry in America. We are more than convinced that the Congress will define objectives which are not yet clear to us; that it will seek to resolve questions we have not yet dared to raise; that new horizons will open for us, and that the new age will begin in Jewish history with its convening.

Therefore, the pulse of Jewry beats so. Therefore the Jewish masses move so. Therefore so much is being done so enthusiastically in Jewish communities in cities large and in towns small.

In Canada, too, various strata of our people have begun to feel the need to unite. In Montreal, Toronto, Ottawa, Quebec, Winnipeg, and elsewhere, there have been set up — or are being set up — committees that strive to do all that is possible to participate in this great, sacred task.

We have therefore come to feel that we must unite all these single trends into one mighty stream which will bear all classes, all parties, all movements in Canadian Jewry to one great political-national act.

Thus, there came into being the idea of the Canadian Jewish Alliance with the following platform: The Alliance seeks to unite Canadian Jewry in the interests of the communal, political and economic responsibilities of the present moment so historic for the Jewish people.

A declaration of principles noted that the condition of the Jews in the countries at war and their fate after the war is the most urgent aspect of the present Jewish reality, and its fundamental and lasting resolution are the sacred duty of the entire Jewish people. The entire history of our nation testifies to the bankruptcy of the practice of intersessionism. The proper resolutions of the Jewish question can be dictated only by the will of the people (...)

The voice of the entire Jewish people is a factor that the great powers will need to take into consideration. This voice is already powerful if only because it is founded upon the right of each people to self-determination. The Jewish people, therefore, needs to formulate its demands. Such possibilities can be created only by peoples' tribunes who come with the directives of the people to deal with the common Jewish interests. Such tribunes can be created only by the purposeful organization and the union of all classes and parties of all tendencies and colorations in the interest of the present great moment. (...)

This peoples' representation must be formed out of the existing religious, political, economic, cultural, welfare, and mutual aid organizations.

Canadian Jews and U.S. Jews
A.M. Mendelbaum
Keneder Odler, October 19, 1915 (?)

As Canadian subjects we should participate in the forthcoming congress; it is of the greatest importance. It is important to determine our position on the questions to be considered at the Congress, for Canadian Jews must bear in mind that Congress will meet in the U.S. and that we differ in some regards from the Jews in the U.S. or in some neutral lands who may attend the Congress. For Canadian Jews are British subjects who are, above all else, loyal to the British flag and conscientiously aware of the interests of our empire.

We shall be very careful that all questions and resolutions that will be considered at the Congress are in accord with our obligation as British subjects. It is therefore of the utmost importance that the leaders of Canadian Jewry, the true representative of every section of the Jewish population of Canada, should attend the Congress, so that the best and most capable forces of Canadian Jewry will join to determine the policies and acts of the Congress.

We call upon the officers of Zionist organizations in every city or district to convene mass meetings of Jews to elect delegates to the conference in Montreal on November 7, 1915.

A Jewish Congress in Canada
Reuben Brainin
Der Veg, November 26, 1915

Our people, which has suffered relatively more than other peoples in the world war, will have to come to the people's *beys din* to demand their honour and their national rights. (...)

American Jews are therefore organizing to hold a Jewish Congress where all classes, all strata, all parties will participate.

The most important Jews of Europe are in favour of a World Jewish Congress, not only an American one. (...) But before such an assembly, the Jews in each country must, wherever possible, have their own national democratic meeting. (...)

(...) [We have issued such a call, a sacred call to Canadian Jews.] And this call has resounded in all Jewish circles in Canada. We have proclaimed a Jewish Congress in Canada, and it must be realized that it must therefore be properly prepared.

We call upon all who favour such a congress to be convened on democratic principles to make this project known in their organizations and in their spheres.

[It] must be discussed from many points of view, and the entire Jewish population must take an interest in it, so that the Congress will become the expression of Canadian Jewry.

Canadian Jewry cannot be excluded from world Jewry. And, as democratic principles are now recognized in the entire world, so we too must fight for these democratic principles in our country.

We, too, cannot permit one class, one party, one group, or a few who have crowned themselves to speak in the name of all Canadian Jewry. (...)

(...) The congress idea must mature and then assume complete expression in reality.

A congress in which all Canadian Jews are represented by their elected delegates will unite the Jewry of this country with the organisms of world Jewry, and then will begin a new epoch of public Jewish life in Canada as well, which may be fated to play a substantial role in the future.

Henceforth, the congress idea must dominate every Jewish gathering in Canada whatever the occasion of its convening. Its warm pulse must be felt in all the movements of public Jewish life.

Our life in this country today is gray, work-a-day and without content, and only a great idea such as the Congress project can give it colour, content, and a measure of sanctity.

The Standstill in the Congress Movement
Yehuda Kaufman
January 10, 1916

This Alliance came in a fortuitous moment of faith in the People's vitality, when what is courageous, beautiful and sacred that was seething in the soul of the people awakened in militant energy, with thirst for acts.

It came in the storm of the cannon in Europe, under the hellish fire of millions of shells flying over the heads and hearts of young Jewish soldiers on all fronts, in the light of Jewish *shtetlekh* being burned and demolished. As brothers and sisters cried out in despair, Canadian Jews began to dream of uniting into a single force to react to the endless persecutions and evil decrees which have already destroyed the major centres and which could, if continued, destroy the entire Remnant of Israel.

We recall the Days of Awe when we created a people's tribune of our representatives who spoke out on the vital problems of the existence of our nation, the belief that in the hour of national danger we could unite to fight for our rights: We are proud to have this Canadian instrument which even the Jews of the United States do not possess.

[Who could have anticipated the national crime which is the arrest of action about the Congress? Not the bitterest enemies of the Congress idea, those few who fought the hundreds of thousands!]

Who, indeed, could have expected such an expiration of such a healthy, mighty people's movement? Our ideologists feared that our politically untrained masses might prove indifferent to the congress idea.(…) [But] our largest numbers had responded to the term "congress" as to a magic revolutionary slogan.(…) It seemed as if a political force not utilized for centuries, dormant deep in the soul of the people, had torn itself away and now was demanding activation in the Congress movement.

The atmosphere about us had become sanctified, as the storekeepers in their shops, women in their kitchen talk, in our great labor associations, or tiny sick benefit societies, in all political organizations, union locals, in chapels and synagogues, everywhere in the greatest and smallest settlements — [all spoke, hoped and dreamed of the Congress,] adopted resolutions about the Messiah-idea of the Congress, [reflecting] the injustices of generations.

Their spines unbent; the language of beggars changed to proud daring demands. What enthusiastic faith and self confidence was implicit in the resolutions formulated in scattered communities consisting of twelve to fifteen families:(…) 'Our Jewish congress shall demand of the Peace Conference of Nations full political and national rights for the Jewish people in the lands of war (…)' and 'the historical rights to Palestine, our home!'(…) One could truly say that the invisible Bastille of Exile had fallen and the entire Jewish people had raised a vast and mighty Flag of Liberty on its ruins. Where are we now with our flag?

Yiddish Versus Hebrew

שרײַבער און לעזער

Reuben Brainin's article, 'Writers and Readers,'
as it appeared in the *Keneder Odler*, January 8, 1913.
(See translation on page 116)
Canadian Jewish Congress National Archives.

THE APPEARANCE OF YIDDISH newspapers in Montreal in the early twentieth century was not without linguistic and political consequences for the ideological struggle in the community over how to maintain Jewish identity in the modern world. Many intellectuals, especially those attached to traditional Zionism, resisted the idea that Yiddish could compete with Hebrew in this sphere and did not want it to hinder the resurgence of Hebrew as part of Jewish nationalism. The coexistence of these two linguistic vehicles on the same political terrain, each carrying a very specific burden of cultural and historical meanings, gave rise to problems that often seemed insoluble. Despite claims of innocence and appeals to the specific Montreal context, publishing a Yiddish paper was in itself equivalent to taking a position in this fierce debate that marked the Ashkenazi diaspora throughout the world.

Some people, like Reuben Brainin, were profoundly convinced that Yiddish was only a *jargon*, a corrupted language reflecting the hard and humiliating conditions imposed on the Jews by their centuries of exile in Christian Europe. Such a language should be used only in situations of great duress, when all other channels of linguistic communication were blocked and the lack of formal education prevented the Jews from attaining the sublime prose of King David and the prophets. This was indeed the case in Montreal, which was receiving thousands of Yiddish-speaking immigrants for whom Hebrew was at best the language of ritual. Most of these newcomers would have been incapable of deciphering the pages of a newspaper written in modern Hebrew. Other people felt that the use of Yiddish was only a stopgap for the uneducated masses newly arrived from European ghettos and that it would quickly be swept away by Canadianization and replaced by English.

Still others, like the Labour Zionists or the Bundists, revered Yiddish as a living expression of the Eastern European Jewish soul, a national language embodying the proletarian revolution and the rising forces in society. For these activists, Yiddish was a weapon in the battle against the forces of religious obscurantism and political reaction, and its rise presaged a new dawn in which the Jewish culture of the *shtetl* would finally take its place in the chorus of modern nations. Whether it was seen as a liberating force, the echo of past humiliations, or simply a necessary step on the way to greater social integration, Yiddish aroused passions in the Montreal Jewish press, especially the Yiddish press, and no one was indifferent to its fate.

Does *Jargon* Have a Future?
I. Yampolsky
Keneder Odler, October 7, 1908

It seems that an examination of the basic question leads to the conclusion that, even if our people will endure, the fate of Yiddish is still problematic.

We nationalists see that our future rests in a distinct territory for our people, whether it be in Palestine or another land. We have no faith in our fate in the lands of exile.

In the lands of exile, it is clear that the assimilatory process works in two directions. In the lands of the half-freedom, such as France, Germany, Italy and Britain, assimilation already crouches on our doorsteps. We are already finished with those born there; they are French Jews, German Jews, British Jews; they are not simply Jews.

As for those who have fled here from these lands of exile, they throw out their infants with the dirty water. They cast out not only Yiddish, but all that is Jewish. In America, from the moment the *griners* first arrive they devote all their efforts to learn English, as if each of them regards Yiddish as a weight on his shoulders; he clings to a Yiddish paper and sometimes he goes to the synagogue, for he remembers the old country. But his children born here are free from this load. They know not a word of Yiddish, have not a touch of religion and nation; they become Americans, not Jews.

It might be argued that we have Yiddish papers, books, theatres, synagogues, study chapels, schools. How can we fear that Judaism is declining?

But why should we deceive ourselves? These institutions are illusory, a candle for extinction, blinking for a moment before it expires. The moment the immigration will cease, they will all expire with the kiss of death, hopefully leaving a monument in Jewish history.

(...) It is futile to hope for a future for our language in the lands of freedom. There remain only our communities in the true exile, in Russia, Romania, Galicia.

Assimilation is at their doorstep, and one need not be a pessimist to see this assimilation devouring the young generation like a flame, scourging the land like a cholera. The young people are adopting the ways and the languages of their country, becoming "free thinkers", in fact, a large percentage cannot speak a single word of Yiddish.

This being the case today, while they are suffering severe discrimination, what will happen to them when they will be partially or fully liberated? And this must come about. The struggle for freedom in Russia must be won and, with the liberty for the Russians, liberty must also come for the Jews there. What will then happen to Yiddish there?

Some will argue that orthodoxy is sufficiently strong there and that many will maintain Yiddish. These need only travel to Hungary to see that as strong as fanaticism may be there, Yiddish is nevertheless totally lost. The classic *Kav Ha Yosher* and *Reshit Khokhma* are studied in German.

So, Yiddish in the free countries has no future. (We do not deny the value of Yiddish as a language and as a contemporary instrument even when we note how it is choked under present conditions).

There remains only the question of which language we shall use in the territory we may hope to acquire.

If this territory is simply a territory, not *Eretz Yisroel*, at the beginning Yiddish may dominate; but it will still meet with stumbling blocks in administration, in foreign affairs. These cannot be conducted in Yiddish. Our own capitalists, aristocrats and intellectuals will not want to use the language.

But if Palestine is our fate, it is barely necessary to recall the likely fate of Yiddish there. The controversy between Herzl and Ahad Ha'am, the spokesmen for the soul of our nation, proves that the linguistic conflict there is so sharp that the outcome is evident even to all who cherish Yiddish.

Clearly we conclude that Yiddish must be seen as the means to our end, and as such it deserves sanctification as the only tongue through which we can reach the masses of our nation, and as the language which carries some original treasures.

But the greatest of these treasures of the Jewish spirit resides in the Hebrew language. Whoever of the *jargon* sages belittles Hebrew deludes himself and his listeners. One page of the Hebrew from Yehudah Halevy and Maimonides to Bialik and Ahad Ha'am is more precious than the entire Yiddish literature, excepting Mendele, and this author is more Hebraist than *jargonist*....Our *jargon* is our contemporary language, but not the language of our future.

On Yiddish
I. Yampolsky
Keneder Odler, November 8, 1908

The masses are largely assimilationist by character, and in our free countries we are losing our populist nature, and Yiddish with it. We are becoming a sect without a confession.

The Hebraists are convinced that an independent Yiddish culture has no foundation in the lands of exile, not even in some arbitrarily selected territory for our people — other than Palestine.

Only there can we have an autonomous language, and that can be only Hebrew; again not because of the efforts of the Hebraists, but because such will be the will of the nation. Hebrew unites the people with its great past, with its sanctities, and must inspire its future.

The Jewish people can have a future only in Palestine. It has a thousand times less future in the exile, and in exile Hebrew has a thousand times less of a future, and Yiddish has a thousand times less of a future.

The Modern Generation of Confusion
Reuben Brainin
Keneder Odler, December 4, 1908

The Jews in the European countries speak all living tongues and even the dialects which dominate their continent. [Yet] they constitute a phenomenon unique among peoples: [they] speak the languages of the world, yet in such unprecedented linguistic wealth our people are so impoverished that we do not have a single living tongue [for common usage for all the nations-in-exile](...) to unite us in all the lands of the dispersion.

As one travels among them from land to land, one experiences the same feeling materially: they are all in exile because they are landless (...) disunited stepchildren even in the land of perfect freedom, even when they do not suffer from practical anti-Semitism (for theoretical anti-Semitism is perpetual, even if in most refined forms). But the native Jews, who are few, have assimilated, at least externally.

Spiritually all Jews are in exile, as they have no language of their own. Everywhere they must speak in alien tongues and when they gather in congress the confusion becomes apparent. I have seen blood-brethren who were brought up in different lands unable to communicate.

I have met Russian immigrants in Paris unable to converse with their children brought up only in French. In four or five years the parents have not acquired French. I have seen Jews who have been in the capital for twenty-five years and know no French. Their children who learn French in school and have been playing with Christian children have forgotten Yiddish (...). I have seen the tragedy in my mother's own home in Vienna and how difficult it was for her to talk with my younger sisters and brothers brought up in German and knowing no Yiddish.

When you see it with your own eyes, you appreciate how much tragedy, how much exile lies in it — how language alienates brothers and parents from children and children from their parents. Among young people born in Russia, Galicia and Romania, I have seen Jews who speak no tongue, not even Yiddish, the *mame-loshn*, who wandered with their parents or without them in country after country in search of repose or sustenance (...) and never stayed anywhere long enough to learn one language; for example they learned German long enough to forget Yiddish, before they were driven to Paris (...) where their baggage of German dissipated and the French which they picked up (...) was of little value to them in England, where they forgot the little French they had, or combined it with some English, etc. (Life knows many such "combinations".) In short, Yiddish they forget almost entirely and their language becomes a mish-mash of tongues, (...) scraps of German, French, English or Dutch, Swedish, Polish, Italian, etc. All these words become twisted and errant in their mouths. Such "cripples in linguism" are increasing in our time (...). We see many polyglot Jews in Western Europe while on the other hand other Jews know no language well.

The only language — our own present Jewish Esperanto — which unites Jews to a degree in various lands to this day is *loshn kodesh*. We can find in every city, in every land, even among the most assimilated, some Jews, (particularly among the rabbis and scholars) with whom we can more or less converse in Hebrew. The genuine French, English, Italian and Spanish know not a word of Yiddish. Where the Jews speak or understand German, (such as in Holland and Scandinavia), Yiddish serves the immigrated Jews from Russia, Galicia and Romania as a means of communicating with the native Jews.

But in Western Europe Yiddish is considered by the locally born as a *jargon* without the right to be considered an independent language. (...) They are "ashamed" of it and hate it when they hear their brethren (in the faith) speak "'Moishe's" tongue, especially in the presence of Gentiles when they seek to earn a living. The new generation of Jews there forget it completely as their elders adopt Yiddish-German, Yiddish-French.

One tells of a Polish Jew who, arriving in Germany; said to a fellow Jew 'The Germans are quite nice people, but the way they speak their language is killing them.'

Of course it is not the Germans that are killed by the language but the Jewish immigrants who come to the country without knowledge of the nation's tongue or tongues, and must suffer materially and spiritually. The refugees must work in Russian-Jewish shops (where Yiddish is spoken), at lower wages. (...)

It is no wonder that these parents strive to have their children correctly learn the language of where they are living. Language courses teach adult immigrants in Berlin and other cities in Germany, like Offenbach and Frankfurt Am Main, in Paris, the "universités populaires," but attendance is not very large. (...)

Intellectual native Jews in Western Europe are distinguished from the gentiles in that they know more languages. (...) That is why most translations in European literature are done by Jews in professions and in offices where the expertise in foreign languages is needed.

Prominent Jews
Dr. Ezekiel Wortsman
Keneder Odler, August 1910

Yiddish literature has come to shine in the endless darkness of our exile life. It is not elevated in its trajectory, not profound in the spirit motivating it. Nevertheless it has brought life into the troubled and pained exile and the freshness of an oasis into the desert of Jewish life.

There may not be unanimity in the faith that Yiddish represents the renaissance of the Jewish people. Geniuses need to arise to dig more deeply in its creative sources to fructify the desert of our culture into a richly planted garden. But certainly the new literature is bringing life and spirit into our poor little world.

It should be dear to every Jew, created as it has been under the most unpromising conditions, in an impoverished and dispirited environment by authors with no material or moral reward. Our youth in particular should reward it by creating a welcoming atmosphere, applaud its writers, disseminate their work. In Russia and in the United States cultural and literary associations study this literature and seek to further its development.

Nowhere is the assimilationist pressure upon our youth as great as in America, threatening our national dignity. Our young must therefore concern themselves with our literature more urgently than anywhere else. The greater the assimilationism the greater must be our resistance. Montreal youth must not lag behind other communities.

Yiddish or Hebrew?
Reuben Brainin
Keneder Odler, September 5, 1912

The conflict between Yiddish and Hebrew, which pits Zionism against the Bund, (...) is a conflict between two conceptions of two worlds, between two Jewish worlds.

One is a world with a future and a past, roots, branches, leaves and fruits. The other is vague exile and a sterile present. (...)

It is good that the conflict is raging.

Regrettably, there are many centres where the conflict never arose. Jews there need neither Yiddish nor Hebrew. Business is conducted in English, and they need neither Talmud Torah nor the Yiddish Peretz Schools.

There is an old fable [that tells of the organs of the body quarrelling as to their primacy]. The feet of a living, healthy man began to quarrel with the hands, saying that without them man could not exist, not walk, not move, and would remain a sort of *golem*. And the hands argued that they are the essential — without them absolutely nothing could be done. The eyes began to fight with the ears, saying that they were the most important, with the ears taking the opposing position. In short, there was a feud between all the limbs and senses of the man, each one thinking itself to be the most important of all.

Where the Jewish organism is sound and vital it can accept both Yiddish and Hebrew and all its spiritual and cultural interests.

When Yiddishists rejoice that Hebrew is forgotten, it is an unhappy joy, as when the feet are happy that the arms are paralyzed, for strength will be sapped from the feet and other [organs] and senses.

More simply, true Hebraists can never hate Yiddish, the language of 95% of the Jews of Russia, Galicia, Britain, and America.

There are Yiddishists who, in their blind fanaticism, hate Hebrew and rejoice in its defeats, but Hebraists love all that the Jewish spirit has created; Yiddish is one such major creation of our spirit.

Writers and Readers
Reuben Brainin
Keneder Odler, January 8, 9 & 17, 1913

Some fifty years ago Hebrew writers arose, took pen in hand to write in all sincerity and with "sacred enthusiasm", under circumstances all their own. [These elite Jewish authors did not even have an audience in these days,] for the Jewish men anxious to learn or to enjoy the arts found their treasures in German or in other European tongues; their own creation had been in sacred works and, even though most of these were in reality great artistic achievements, they were read as if they were only liturgical in function.

[Before that time Jews had no authors,] i.e. writers who live in contemporaneity, relate to their people, influence their people, teach their people. This type emerged with the press during the past twenty-five years, in Yiddish and Hebrew twins. As stalks on a single stem, most great literary talents work in both the Hebrew and the Yiddish press — each writer with his public, his circle of influence, with his readers who have learned to understand him and to honour and love him.

[The Jewish author has faith in the infinite potential of the Jewish masses as he draws his force, his purification from the Jewish people. Without such a sense of the genuineness of the large masses of the people, the author could not write every day and could not teach and encourage his readers.]

Each day he is weakened, his strength disappears altogether. [The people sense instinctively who is close to him and who will be faithful to the last moment; and the author who speaks to him each day is not chosen by election or by a higher authority. Only his God-given awareness, energy and call turn the ardent love of his suffering kin into the people's thinker and ultimate leader, crowned by the people.]

[January 17, 1913] (...)A Jewish author with talent, spirit and creative ability — not to speak of character, personality, consistency and purity of soul — was recognized in all spheres and classes and became beloved of the people, even a popular hero.

(...)Our people are poor in great spirits who remain true to our nation, who create for our people and with our people; it is therefore a crime to limit them and to stifle them within the bounds of the group.

The Sons of My Generation: Deeds and Events
Torn Pages from my Diary and Notes
that Derive from the Heart
Reuben Brainin
Keneder Odler, March 20, 1913 (?)

Today there appeared as supplement to the *Odler* the Hebrew literary pages, which I composed and edited. It is a slight contribution, because the Passover issue which I issued was trilingual: in Hebrew, Yiddish, and English. But this is precisely the first Hebrew edition in literary Hebrew. I succeeded in this experiment after much effort.

I worked on it day and night. I edited, wrote, corrected, explained to the typesetters and the compositors to produce the text I desired, in spite of all obstacles, for the machines and printers, messengers and proof-readers are all accustomed to the Yiddish. The appearance of this Hebrew text has been a matter of miracle.

Am I happy? No, for this sheet is alone in Hebrew, and its readers are few and isolated.

On the Merits of Hebrew
Reuben Brainin
Presumed to be from his diary, circa 1913

Hebrew has concentrated the elements of the vitality of the Jewish people, the originality of its power, the secrets of its existence. I sense in this language the soul and uniqueness of the People and the Land of Israel where it was born, matured, developed, and flowered magnificently. When I speak Hebrew I sense my own pride in its sound and its strength, its finesse, delicacy, clarity and elegance.

Even as I speak it I hear the echoes of the renewed culture of its ancient composers, philosophers, prophets. My words and the words of my interlocutors are related, linked to the heritage of my past and to the continuity of our future. If I suffer for a term to perfect my expression, I know that behind me and at my side are our literatures with inexhaustible vocabularies where all of us become treasure hunters. Then my words are born in royal purple as are my brothers.

The Yiddish Theatre

Keneder Odler, April 22, 1910.
An advertisement (corner, upper left) announces the appearance
of Madame Rose Karp at the Monument National Theatre
during Passover.
Canadian Jewish Congress National Archives.

THE ADVENTURE of Yiddish theatre in Montreal began in 1897 at the Monument National theatre on St. Lawrence Boulevard when Isaac Zolotarevsky presented a Yiddish adaptation of Shakespeare's *King Lear*. As Israel Medres recalls in his memoir, *Montreal fun Nekhtn*, this was the start of an art form that was to bring large Jewish crowds to the Monument National for over half a century, captivating a community for whom the great Yiddish actors were individuals of exceptional artistic and human stature. Year after year, local troupes or those from New York presented the major plays of the Yiddish repertoire in Montreal and brought the most distinguished actors to the Montreal stage.

While the Montreal community was agreed as to its importance as an art form, Yiddish theatre nonetheless aroused fierce debate in the local press. Should plays with the loftiest writing and sentiments be given precedence or, on the other hand, should the theatre aim to attract a larger public by presenting mediocre plays in which the expression of feeling was crude and the characters often mawkish. Was there a place for *shund*, or more vulgar plays, at the Monument National, or should the impresarios' efforts to fill the theatre at any cost be condemned? There were also discussions of specific interpretations, the tone used by an actor, or the quality of the direction. The following four articles show the kinds of issues that concerned the journalists of the *Keneder Odler*.

Yiddish Theatre
Author unknown
Presumed to be in *Keneder Odler*, 1909

Until recently Montreal was able to boast to other provincial cities of having had Yiddish plays. It did not have a permanent theatre, but it could see the best productions of the Yiddish repertoire by the best New York actors.

We always respected the efforts of our theatre manager to provide us with the best New York plays and we supported him in not sparing expenses to bring in the best actors, and thus winning the recognition of all to whom Yiddish culture, and particularly Yiddish theatre, are dear in raising the spiritual lives of our people.

Truth to tell, we were not particularly overjoyed to hear of the founding of a permanent Yiddish company and the mobilizing of a company of actors. Such a project might benefit the managers but not the general public.

True, until now, we have enjoyed but three performances a month, but we had quality. A permanent group might give us three shows a week, but we would (not) be fed particularly clean or healthy food.

It is impossible that such notably distinguished actors could be secured by the local theatre managers, nor would it pay them. With weak actors they could present but weak plays, or bury good plays.

We were therefore highly satisfied that nothing came of the permanent Yiddish theatre in Montreal.

The failure of the plan did not save us from vulgarity or poor actors.

During the last few months Montreal has not seen Odler or Kessler or Mme. Liptzin. We have not seen a single more or less literary play. We have been fed with various Simons and Silberts, with *Yeshivah Students* and *Queen of Shebas*, with actors deserving criticism; instead of the dramas we have had Purim plays and clowning. Suddenly, our theatrical management has gone twenty years backward, from Goldfaden, when a good comedian was the best that our repertory possessed, where the public cracked peanuts and neither the actor nor the public respected each other.

Possibly our theatrical management has altered its tactic, for the more recent productions of the better New York companies have not been successful. But management should have understood that the crisis is at fault, as is evidenced by the more recent cheap productions that were not particularly successful.

But even if management found it profitable to produce on the yellow stage, it is not profitable for those who attend theatre, and we shall protest this strongly.

We are informed that we shall be presented the same Silbert-Simon Company. We counsel the local management not to pursue this line. The bad times will slowly pass and we hope we will enjoy success. May the management revert to its old program!

Our Theatre
Reuben Brainin
Keneder Odler, February 16, 1912

Every people has the theatre it deserves. It is not a gift from heaven or a lottery ticket.

Drama is the ripest fruit of the higher culture of a people. The theatre and its condition is the spiritual barometer of a people. It indicates its cultural development, the refinement of its taste, its aesthetic sense, the depth of its spiritual needs.

And here comes the sad question: Does the Jewish people stand so low? For we must admit that the Yiddish theatre stands at a very low level, and will not rise; it will not develop, it will not refine, improve and whenever one takes a step forward, takes two steps backwards. How come?

As a whole, the entire Jewish people is more literary, more sensitive, more aesthetic, more understanding, with a keener appreciation of the art of the stage and the theatre than many cultured nations. It has produced among the most dramatic artists. It is established that Jews generally attend the best non-Jewish art theatres, more than one purely artistic theatre, and that in Germany theatre could not develop without Jewish artists and talented directors and audiences; in short, without material assistance and social aid.

So how is it that the Jewish theatre, the youngest child of the Jewish people, is so pale, so bloodless, bare skin and bones, so without real life, so without real desire to live or capacity to live, or capacity for development? Speaking openly and honestly, the weakness of Yiddish theatre is a sign of the poverty of our people.

How is it that Yiddish theatre has the ugly habit of locking the door to its true dramatic talents, to its literary powers, to the cleaner more original and higher art except when they bend and suppress their talent perforce, mask their intent with the clownish or with (...) banality.

How is it that we have, on one side talented playwrights, stage artists and actors who are tortured with plays which have no genuine types, no consistent characters, where the Jewish actors cannot demonstrate the nuances of their talent and have no possibilities to develop it; and on the other side, the managers of the Jewish theatres suspect and show fear of new, good pieces and talented and earnest playwrights?

These striking contradictions can be explained by many varying, distant and immediate causes. We will pause at one: the Jewish intellectuals, those who wish to be counted among them, the uptowners, or those who strive there, speak American. Most Jews who understand more or less English turn their head from the Yiddish theatre and neither want to see or hear of it. It is beneath their dignity.

Mr. L. Mitnick, who knows the Jewish stage and the Jewish public well, and has much experience, founded a permanent Yiddish theatre in Montreal and exerted all efforts to create a Yiddish stage with talented artists in the fine spacious Monument National, a Yiddish theatre which is peerless outside New York. Outside the permanent talented group which is playing this winter in the Monument National, Mr. Mitnick brings various stars, the greatest Jewish players which America possesses.

We criticized strongly some vulgar plays in the Monument National not only in our newspapers but also in private conversation. Each time we brought to his attention that the average intelligence in Montreal is much superior to the New York equivalent.

I have attempted several times to convince Mr. Mitnick, who always wishes to present only the best artistic productions in his theatre, with the aid of the best performers, that even on the material side it pays to present more literary, more artistic pieces.

Mr. Mitnick provided me with a practical answer.

This winter he performed the best dramas, *God, Man and the Devil* (where Isidore Meltzer played Leiser Badchen magnificently), and the theatre gallery was full, but down below and in the boxes a goodly crowd might have attended. In short, a failure.

On the contrary, in the presentation of what in my language I called "idealistic vulgarity" the theatre was packed, and we had to repeat the performances, and the Montreal audience enjoyed it every time.

After such examples Mr. Mitnick asked me each time, 'What now? Do you still say that the Jewish public of Montreal which frequents the theatre is ready for good artistic plays?'

I am still of the opinion that the more intelligent Jewish audience in Montreal can fill the Monument National several times a month and leave large numbers outside the hall to see our artistic work, and the test is set.

Mr. Mitnick will perform on February 22, the newest comedy by our most original state artist, Peretz Hirshbein, at the Monument National. He has just completed a masterpiece of a comedy, *The Obscure Corner,* with its premiere in Montreal.

Hirshbein is the most sympathetic and original dramatic talent in Yiddish literature. His plays are translated into Russian and evoke enthusiastic criticism and are being successfully played on the Russian stage.

We hope and believe that the Jewish public of Montreal will know how to appreciate this first performance of Hirshbein's new work in our city.

On February 22, the Jewish art lovers, the readers of our literature, and amateurs of (...) Montreal will respond. Can we pack the Monument National only when we present a nameless work by an author without a name or sense, but with song and dance, and no room for a Peretz Hirshbein, one of the great creators of Jewish art and culture?

The people's theatre lies in the hands of the public.

On the Yiddish Theatre Debate
Isaac Yampolsky
Presumed to be in *Keneder Odler,* 1912

(...) Which, together with its ubiquitous manager Mr. Mitnick, is undergoing a psychological experience which will need resolution in the future.

Simply, the public is protesting; they do not go to the theatre. The actors perform to bare walls. Mitnick orates to no listeners. He applies the full force of his ambition to impose the dramatic diet which he would prescribe. His foolish ambition has fallen to indecency. He condemns the writers or the writers who criticized his first production and stamps all intellectuals in shameful terms which are proper to market women rather than to a theatrical manager. Of course, the consequence of such anger is more foolishness and impudence rather than consideration.

We would pose him some questions if he is in a state to consider anything serious.

Do you really believe that the empty theatre is the result of the writings of the critics who have only asked you not to feed your audience with vulgarity? After all, you did promise them literature. If this is so, you should appreciate the *Odler*'s sincerity.

But we see things differently. We see the empty theatre not as a consequence of the critics' comments but as a result of your policy. The newspaper is but the mirror of the sense of the people.

You claim that the public seeks vulgarity rather than art. You claim that you give the public what they want. That is not true. The theatres are empty when you present vulgarity or art. Nor is it up to you to decide, as a man in business, what to show.

The theatre is not yours. You did not create the theatre. In that sense the writers have more rights than you do and all the theatrical managers of America. It was the Yiddish writers, with their blood of thirty years, who created the Yiddish stage. Sad as it may still be, it is a product of Jewish thinkers. It takes impertinence to degrade them from the Yiddish stage.

It is our theatre, Mr. Mitnick; your insults will certainly not frighten us.

(Untitled)
Ben Bzalel
Keneder Odler, November 13, 1912

At one time Siebel was performing in the Palace and Mme. Prager in the Monument National. The Palace engaged the Misses Odler. Mitnick is not satisfied with mere stars and will probably bring down the moon, and the Palace will be forced to bring the Zodiac.

If you believe that the Montreal public is at the same level as it was thirty years ago, you are making a grave error which you will appreciate sooner than you expect. How can so experienced a manager know his public so poorly? Whatever led him to think it wants such a vulgar piece as *Money, Love and Shame* by Zolotarevsky? Would you want your daughter to hear Meltzer's bawdy song or Miss Hoffman's nigger verse?

Mr. Mitnick, you must stop this. The public will not bring their children, their sisters, their wives or their mothers. They will learn that movies are better and cheaper.

You presented a program which was an offence to an intelligent audience. It is an insult to Montreal Jewry to call it the Montreal Jewish Theatre. Instead of this theatre — rather nothing.

The actors are young. The seeds of talent which some of you possess will be choked by your ignorance. Are you actors or vaudeville performers?

On French Canada

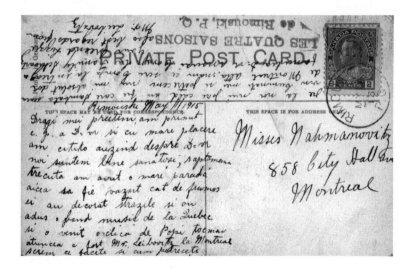

Postcard sent May 1915 by a Romanian Jewish immigrant
living in Rimouski, Québec. It describes recent events in the town.
Canadian Jewish Congress National Archives.

AT FIRST GLANCE, in the early years of the twentieth century the French fact does not appear to have been of particular concern to the Montreal Yiddish press. The Yiddish-speaking Jews, striving to adapt to their material and human situation in their new country, quickly understood that English was economically and politically dominant in Canada and generally did not learn French, especially because the Catholic school authorities refused for religious reasons to allow them to attend French-language public schools. During the early years, therefore, contact between the linguistic majority and the eastern European immigrants was quite limited, particularly in the institutional sphere, so much so that very few Yiddish-speakers read the French press, took part in French-Canadian cultural activities, or met any prominent French-speaking Quebecers.

However, occasionally, someone wiser and better able to master languages would break through the barrier separating Francophones and Yiddish-speakers. This was the case of the young Roback, who served as the fourth editor-in-chief of the *Keneder Odler* from 1911 to 1912 and who, unusually for the time, had a university education. Such encounters sometimes had extraordinary consequences; for example, in 1912, at the time of a major conference on the French language in Quebec City, Roback published an article praising French-Canadian nationalism. From there it was only a small step to making a comparison with the fragile state of the Yiddish language in Montreal and the half-hearted attachment of certain Canadian Jews to their heritage, a step that Roback did not hesitate to take. A similar admiration is expressed at the same time by the columnist and historian B.G. Sack, who also notes how deeply the conference of 1912 marked what was the cultural and political life of French Canada of the time.

In a similar vein, a 1916 piece by H.M. Caiserman, a prominent trade unionist and cultural activist in Montreal in this period, speaks of Ontario's Regulation 17 against the teaching of French as a ukase wrongfully imposed on the French-speaking population of the province. Standing up for the minority, Caiserman supported the struggle of Henri Bourassa and the Quebec nationalists for cultural and linguistic freedom in Canada just as he supported the struggle of the left-wing Jews in the czarist empire during the same period. While these articles on the French-speaking people of Quebec may seem isolated and even incongruous in the pages of the *Keneder Odler* or *Der Veg* in the early years of the century, they nonetheless foreshadow developments of great importance that took place in the thirties, when Yiddish-speakers gradually came into greater contact with their counterparts in the majority and learned through this contact to better gauge their own place in Quebec society.

A Lesson from the French
A.A. Roback
Keneder Odler, July 7, 1912

The French press customarily points to the Jews as an example: We do not drink, do not overspend, work our way up, are united with iron steel.

Even the anti-Semitic press writes this about us, and by and large it is true that our drunkards are as few as are our criminals, our people climb from the lower class. What does this mean? Simply that as individuals we stand above them. The compliment is undeserved.

But as we regard the French as a people we need not be ashamed of them as a group (...). In terms of nationalism we are decades behind them. In Canada there are two million of them under difficult circumstances. Ignorance hampered the spiritual development of the province composed largely of 80% French. But their nationalism grew constantly. No need to awaken them with bells and have them return to their deep sleep, as may be our case. Nationalism among the French, in whose midst we live, is deeply rooted. Every one of them, no matter how ignorant he is, is aware of his language, and they fight a battle for it, in spite of unpleasantness, to prevent having the English gain strength at the cost of French.

(...) They distinguish between themselves as Canadians, and the English here as persons, who are only residing here. They refuse to identify as members of one people who share one common Canadian nationhood. A Jew will always bear in mind his common national identity and the land where he was born; they speak of Heine as a German poet, of Bergson as a French philosopher; they will tell of them except when they whisper, 'But he is a Jew.'

In the English schools, the French children speak French even though all their studies were conducted in English schools. When a Jewish student speaks Yiddish with a Jewish colleague, people look askance at him.

(...) A detail: visit a picture or book auction.The book or art work displaying life in a French village or in French colony will fetch any price, regardless of their artistic value. The national value determines. But our wealthy houses do not need these rags which portray the sabbath afternoon, a Friday night, a *yeshiva* of scholarly debate. There is no displaying such portrayals. These Jews have seen the Madonna, the Venus, Rembrandt and they buy them. What have they to do with unquestionable Jewish life? There is, naturally, no national Jewish life, only minimizing the master of the house.

But these are all details compared to the great congress for the promotion of French speech in our country (Congrès de la langue française).

It is truly remarkable. As we have noted: The French Canadians will speak only French, and never in English to anyone even though they themelves can speak English perfectly. But as soon as French intellectuals noted the rise of English they convened a congress with rare enthusiasm to appeal to their people to speak only their language. The bishops, the writers, the statesmen and all the subjects of His Majesty spoke up in defence of French, to recognize it as well as English as the language of the country. The premier of an English province (Sir Lomer Gouin) encouraged his colleagues to speak only in their own tongue. What a pleasure to hear those words from the premier of Quebec: "This language which we learned at our mother's hands deserves every sacrifice, every effort, the erection of academia, colleges and schools where our children can learn, together with English, all the beauties of sweet French." (...)

The Church and the French Language in Canada
B.G. Sack
Presumed to be in *Keneder Odler* July, 1912

It was an extraordinary event in the history of not only the province but the whole land, with philosophic English, and French, and moral significance in the relations of the two ruling nationalities in the land which sought to limit the peaceful yet dangerous competition between them. (...)

[In this context the clerical element is the most effective force as an international institution, champion and initiator of the language, (...) possibly with its own interest of French purity and character, (...) under the slogan, "Language and Faith". The language is the defender of the Catholic religion, (...) even as it emerges, as the francophones cannot live as a nation without their language. The two (...) cannot live without each other.]

The Catholic church was established at first only in French, thus it was first planted, it built a fortress across the nation (...).

The Catholic church recognizes that its vitality depends upon the strength of the French in the country (...). The language is the only instrument against assimilation with the English, which would mean a loss of their influence, and therefore the defence of the language is the strongest among the French nationalists and the clerical elements (...). Both cooperate intimately.

Whether the continuation of the French language in Canada is dependent upon the Catholic church is another question. The answer is most definitely the negative.

But the francophone Congress carries a tremendous purely cultural significance. (...) We shall deal with this again in a second article.

My Voyages in Canada
Philip Krantz
Presumed to be in *Keneder Odler,* August, 1915

French Canadians hope that immigration from Italy, Poland and other Catholic lands will increase the power of the church which is more influential in French Quebec than anywhere else.

In any case, French has been spoken in the St. Lawrence Valley for centuries. No matter how strong the English element will grow, the fruitfulness of the French Canadians will always give them greater natural strength.

The red thread — coloured red for blood — of English-French conflict runs throughout the entire history of Canada, in a variety of forms; it will never cease as long as the habitants of Canadian villages will speak and study French.

This will not slow the further growth of all Canada as it did not in the nineteenth century.

On Labour Zionism and the Bund
H.M. Caiserman
Der Veg, February 11, 1916

(...)I conclude that both ideologies are sisters in the blood, and that they differ only in that the Bundists had left their nationalism in Russia. And here [in Canada] their nationalism consists of combatting any form of national unification and impeding any practical activity of a national character; whereas the Poale Zion socialists remained more or less true to their program. Why is this so? Is the struggle of a class for its free expression more important than the struggle of a whole oppressed people for the freedom to think and to speak? If a strike of ten workers is important enough for socialists to help them, is it not insane to believe that the struggle of an entire people which seeks to free itself is not worthy of this help?

If the socialist cannot reach the masses of the Jewish people with his ideas, he must study Jewish psychology, which differs from that of other people, and adjust socialism to the Jewish environment, to language and customs which have developed in a long historical process — so it happened in our history and in other histories. We have never had socialism on the Jewish street (...) as long as socialism was "translated." Socialism became the religion of the Jewish masses when it grew out of the innermost of our own life. [this has been the greatest and most important national achievement of the Bund.](...) Socialism [although the same doctrine] is today in all countries, according to the temperaments and national qualities of each people. (...)

If socialism could develop itself on national foundations, (...) and could in turn, deliberately or otherwise, develop national cultures, it is not its elementary duty [as a liberation movement] to mobilize for complete national freedom for two major reasons: first in the interests of freedom proper and second to bring a democratic element into nationalism. For can the conscious socialist deny that every struggle of the oppressed nations is a struggle for freedom, and even more a struggle for democracy? And if this is so can the socialist fail to support any battle for liberation, not only by programs but by vivid action?

(...)Is it not clear how much socialism can add to such a nationalism where so many active elements lie so clearly to hand? Until the war the Poale Zion were the only socialists who were positive towards nationalism.

The Socialist International paid for this short sightedness with its [very] existence: (...)[it led to the bankruptcy of the International because of its negative stand on the national question.]

It is clear that Jewish socialists should open their eyes.(...)

We can ask whether the struggle for the nation is in the interests of democracy. A vivid example] is being played out before our eyes in the Ontario language war. The population of the province is Catholic, that is, people who do not cease to speak of the People and God. The majority of them are anglophone and the minority, francophone. According to the Montreal Capitulation and the Quebec Act and later the "Act of 1763" and finally the "British North America Act", the French language shares equality with English. But the English majority wishes to impose its culture and language upon the French, and contrary to the spirit of the constitution they concocted "Regulation 17" in August 1913 which, in Russian style, would revoke from the French the right to educate their children as they wish.

Along came French Canadian nationalists headed by Bourassa (Catholics holier than the Pope) who set aside the famed Catholic solidarity to lead a truly wondrous, courageous and anti-patriotic battle for the cultural liberty of the minority. The national struggle stands above religion and when religion stands in the way of democracy it must be set aside.

Do the Jewish socialists believe that such a struggle deserves support of all right thinking people?

Reminiscences

Discussion outside Harry Hershman's newsstand, 1906.
Photo by W. Sharp, Montreal Standard.
Canadian Jewish Congress National Archives.

AMONG THE DOCUMENTS in the collection left by David Rome as part of this project were a certain number of texts written in either Yiddish or English and published in a later period than that of the great migration of 1905 to 1914. Most of them are articles written by immigrants to Montreal in the early twentieth century who are looking back thirty or forty years to this exceptional time in Quebec Jewish history. These were people who were mostly either too young in the key years of eastern European immigration or not yet influential enough in the community to have put their impressions down on paper. Several decades later, these firsthand witnesses have a better understanding of the importance of the events they experienced, and they want the upcoming generation to be aware of the historical distance travelled in Montreal since the Russian insurrection of 1905.

Three of these chroniclers stand out for the richness and range of their writing: Israel Medres, Simon Belkin, and Hirsch Hershman. The first two wrote memoirs that place them in the first rank of Yiddish-speaking historians of their community, while Hershman's writing took a more literary direction, in poetry, short stories and essays. In 1947, Medres published *Montreal fun Nekhtn* (*Montreal of Yesterday: Jewish Life in Montreal, 1900-1920* [Montréal: Véhicule Press, 2000]), about the wave of immigration at the beginning of the century and the early days of the Jewish community in the city. Belkin in 1956 published *Di Poale-Zion Bavegung in Kanade, 1904-1920* (The Labour Zionist Movement in Canada, 1904-1920), which traces the development of Labour Zionism, an ideology that was very important in Canadian Jewish history.

David Rome undoubtedly wanted to include these texts in his proposed collection for the Canadian Jewish Congress to show the contrast between writings from the turbulent period of immigration, which are marked by daily struggle, and those from much later, written in a spirit of nostalgia and benign commemoration. This contrast brings out the unique-ness of the *Keneder Odler* pieces written at the time, and their role in the immigrants' struggle to adapt to a new social environment and new working conditions in a highly industrialized society.

Main Street
Esther Kershman Muhlstock
Unpublished in Yiddish version, circa 1988.
Modified version published, in English, in
Canadian Jewish Outlook, Jan/Feb. 1990.

(...) for me and my first generation of the young days of the twentieth century, in memories and yearnings, all our paths lead to the important street of my youth, "Main Street." The whole street and area was like one family. Everyone knew all the good news to the minute and sympathized with the bad news. People helped each other.

On Main Street all the merchants knew us. For this reason we children stole an apple from the stalls: an apple here, a pear there. Who does not know the taste of a stolen apple? Especially a sour, hard apple. It is the taste of *Gan-Eden*. It almost freezes the tongue: a tasty bite.

We bought our textbooks from Lazarus Book Store near Roy Street, on the Main. Books, books, books, books from floor to ceiling: books in every corner with a high ladder by the wall to reach a book up high.

Men, young and old, some well dressed, others in old or torn clothes (who cared?), some shaven, others bearded, some unemployed, some who dropped in after work for an hour to meet friends, to take part in a discussion: every summer and winter sitting, standing around a small heater with a big belly, learning the latest news, a reading by a poet, sitting, when possible, on crates, benches or the floor.

These were the founders of the institutions of our time: our "Caisermans", our "Dicksteins", our library, our *gmiles khsodim*, our immigrant association, our Peretz School, our People's Schools, our "Baron de Hirsch", and other Jewish organizations. These were men of initiative, of social feeling and far-seeing plans. People of culture, not learning, people with ideals: Zionists, Poale Zionists, Zeirei Zionists, religious, not pious, all sorts of people who believed, hoped, worked for a healthy Jewish environment in their new home in Montreal, in Canada.

The storekeepers along the Main sold anything a person could want. They filled all demands and dreams: golden jewellery (...), a warm fur coat? As well as chickens, ducks, geese, fruits, greens, dishes from old Poland, Romania, Austria and other cities, a transplantation of the *shtetl* into Canada and Montreal.

The people were entranced by the street, so full of character, friendship and hominess. One heard spoken a variety of tongues. They bargained heartily with the merchants but the mood was always good (...), unhurried. Everyone enjoyed themselves. The sidewalks were full of people pushing each other. Four in line, arm in arm, letting no one pass. A child is lost. People hug her, kiss it, someone offers her a candy, "Don't cry, Mother will come soon."

Near Duluth on Main Street was the Bernstein store: clothing, underwear for children and adults. We were seven children (...). Only at Bernstein's could we buy winter underwear. One pair per child, (two for Daddy), winter caps, cold weather underclothing with ribbons for us [three girls], on layaway (one dollar a week) payments. (Who had enough money to pay all at once?) All were satisfied. Mr. Bernstein did business. 'Take, take' he would urge on my mother. 'I will see you on Sunday, we will straighten it out.'

Sunday came. Mr. Bernstein also. And not only him, but the butcher, the "syphon" man, and who else? I do not remember them all, but I remember that Sunday night there was not enough money for the week. We were not exceptional. No one had money. 'As long as I have a few pennies for a poor man,' my mother comforted herself.

A few steps from Bernstein's (...) was our pride, our *Keneder Odler*. The *Keneder Odler* and the *Bintl Briv* [the "mail bundle" column] in the *Forvertz*: this was the literature for the week. Adjoining the *Odler* was Horn's Cafeteria, open all night, where the editors and staff of the printshop would engage in discussing their hot themes over a glass of tea or coffee 'till they had to return to work in their interesting world.

(...) The world of the talented artists, gifted sculptors (...), inventors with modern ideas, men like Bercovitch, Fainmel, Bader, our young artists fresh from Paris with new influences: all around the fat-bellied heater at Mayman's paint store on Main Street past Prince Arthur.

Some came in to warm up from the cold, to use the washroom, or grab a bite to chase off hunger, or exchange a few words with Mr. Mayman about complaints against the world; some sought inspiration, advice or a bed to sleep in. His door was always open, to Jew or Christian. (...)

How can one end with Main Street and not tell about the Monument National Theatre, on the Main near St. Catherine? About the plays, actors, crowds, tears and laughter — how one feels in a Yiddish theatre among Jewish people and the Jewish mother tongue! How good we had it!

My childhood years were good and fine and bourgeois. A wonderful education, a feeling for everyone, a rich influence on my whole life (...).

Montreal: How the Immigrants
Found An Intellectual Atmosphere
Israel Medres
Canadian Jewish Chronicle, April 3, 1936

It was on Main Street near St. Catherine Street that Hershman's Book Store was located, and the intellectuals would gravitate towards this centre to find the appropriate atmosphere. For them, Hershman's Book Store was a cultural centre where one could obtain a variety of journals and books. The true immigrant type, however, was satisfied with buying a glass of soda water which fizzed from a mysterious faucet for a cent a glass. While observing this regular routine he would buy his newspaper, and, if he were successful enough to look forward to a pay-day, he would buy an occasional book.

Many of these books were *romanen*, sentimental love stories which appeared in the Old Country in serial form and which so delighted the hearts of the housewife and maid. There would also be found a type of book which had a medical aspect to it, purporting to give advice to young men, maidens, and young wives. Such literature was unknown to the immigrant in his old home-town. But there were also to be found books by modern writers, to say nothing of anarchistic propaganda literature.

However, Hershman's was not the only cultural rendezvous with Yiddish atmosphere. On Main street there were (...) three between St. Catherine and Ontario Streets, each of them a common meeting-place for the *kultur* seekers among the immigrant youth. No matter at what hour a person would enter these stores, he would be sure to find little groups discussing and arguing the philosophies of life.

Each store had its specialty on the line of "cultural dissemination." In one place the favourite theme might be anarchism, due no doubt to the prevalence of anarchistic pamphlets and literature on the shelves. The store-keeper was himself a specialist in this line of literature, and he would shrewdly try to convey the impression that he is an idealist who is devoting himself to the "cause" rather than a materialist who sold all branches of literature. When the store-keeper was asked for a glass of soda water or a package of cigarettes by a customer he would take his time and lend an ear to the discussions that were being waged, throwing in his comment as well. The cigarettes could wait while he championed the teachings of Karl Marx, Peter Kropotkin, Rudolf Rocker, Johan Most, or Emma Goldman if it were necessary. The cigarettes or soda water could wait still longer while the erudite store owner would take a book down from his shelf in order to support his contentions.

These debates were particularly lively when *Erev Yom Tov* came around. On *Erev Pesach*, for instance, one would hear excited discussions as to whether a radical youth, living with religious parents, should sit at the *seder* table to placate his folks, or should his ideology stand supreme even at the risk of quarrelling with his family. On *Erev Yom Kippur* the subject for debate would be whether true anarchists should stage an anti-religious demonstration by means of a dance, or a feast in a restaurant, or ignore the event completely.

The Jewish immigrant intelligentzia stood in wonderment before such discussion. To him it was a puzzle that in the great America, where there is so much freedom and worldly goods for all, there should be the need for allotting such an important place to such extreme theories as anarchism. (...)

Bit by bit, however, he became accustomed to these manifestations of eloquence and their theories.

Many of these one-time anarchists, who would spend hours in the book shops every day and argue the pros and cons (mostly pros) of anarchism, are today busily engaged looking after thriving businesses which they have, in the course of time, built for themselves. They are today the proprietors of large stores and factories, and many of them have now a greater hatred for extreme radicalism than what they once had for the capitalist system.

Discussions in book shops were not the only outlets for the mental energy of the youthful immigrant intellectuals. They would often bring in lecturers from New York, many of whom were known as authors of socialist and anarchist pamphlets, or contributors to the pages of radical dailies.

The *Forverts* Among the Jewish Masses of Canada
Hirsch Hershman
Forverts, May 25, 1947

[In Montreal, unlike my New York condition,] I had enough, almost too much free time. I, however, did not have what to do with this free time. I had nowhere to turn for intellectual satisfaction. The community consisted of several thousand souls, but no sign of cultural life, especially for anyone who had spent several years in New York in a more or less cultural sphere (...).

East Europe supplied the proletariat for the several tailor shops, managed more or less well by former immigrants from Russia, Poland, Lithuania and Romania.

The East European immigrants of the time earned their livelihood in the penny trade, peddling from house to house with a basket of "junk ware": candles, knives, needles and thread, or as petty merchants. The more daring set out over the province to peddle among the French farmers.

During these years the population in the roads and villages of the province, in the faraway corners, had little contact with the outside world. They generally were worried, stooped Jews with the experience of millennia exile in their tired eyes, bent by packs of heavy merchandise on their shoulders, seeking their bread in sign language. The peddlers would return to the city only to refresh their stocks, which consisted of the usual home-articles that a farmer would need. They would then head out again to wander over the scattered muddied dirt roads of the province and knock on peasants' doors.

Many of these travellers in the remote regions where they peddled would receive their goods by rail from the big city to avoid loss of time and travel costs to Montreal. The city interested them little, having no one close to them there and no public life of interest to them. As such, they would come to Montreal for Passover or the High Holy Days.

I believe there is in a general way to be seen a social problem with which the young country peddler was met during his wanderings in the province of Quebec. The absence of a Jewish environment and constant contact with French farmer families was a regular occurrence, so that a young Jewish peddler could fall in love with, and marry, a French girl, and so he is torn away from his roots. As a member of the French Canadian family, where he was readily accepted, he would in time establish himself in business in the province and become an established member of society. Never converting, perish the word, or even changing his name, he became transformed into a "Canadien français". As such, he was drawn into the sea of assimilation. All because Montreal, the only Jewish centre in Canada, was unattractive, socially, for the newcomer of the time. That is why there developed in Quebec many French Canadian families with the names of Levy, Vosberg, Flashman and David, the heirs of the Jewish country peddlers of half a century ago.

(...) While my friends were discussing theoretical questions, I looked into bringing the printed socialist word into Montreal. I soon saw that their meager yet heated debates on Karl Marx's *Communist Manifesto* and the *Socialist Trade and Labour Alliance* will not enlighten the Jewish workers of Montreal. I argued with my wife that the printed word appeals to the worker, even without the eloquence. She agreed with me. We decided to create readers for the *Forvertz*. (...) Three dollars for a subscription was too great a price for a worker to pay all at once, but seven cents a week would find interest. And I was not mistaken. I sent to New York for a number of copies, and I would deliver them evenings for my subscribers.

The enlargement of my paper route led me to open a small store which also sold socialist pamphlets from New York as well as the London *Fraync* and whatever else appeared of socialist enlightenment, and the work of the young Yiddish creators whom the *Forvertz* then discovered and introduced to the Jewish readers. So I became the first Jewish bookseller in Montreal.

The undertaking was almost incidental, but this soon altered for it became the centre of the Jewish labour movement in our city, the centre of the *Forvertz* in Montreal.

This came in 1903. The pogroms in Kishinev, in Homel and elsewhere in Russia created a great Jewish migration from the Czar's empire of such elements who had never before thought of changing their homes for America.

The major stream was drawn to the United States, but Canada received a share. The Jewish population of Montreal began to grow in numbers and, even more important, in quality. Suddenly our meeting came to see new visitors with whom we did not need to begin the ABC but who had passed stages of European socialist and revolutionary movement. They brought a new spirit into our meetings. The discussions became livelier, more interesting and better attended.

The new Jewish immigrants increased until the First World War. The greatest influx of Jews in Canada came from 1904 to 1908 because of events in Russia. The war with Japan, the unrest after Russia's defeat and its capitulation, the pogroms which the government had prepared to cover the shame of its defeat — these stormy events in Russia brought to Canada a fresh stream of Jewish immigrants, many of them disappointed with the failure of the Revolution.

This stream was accompanied by many Jewish wanderers from Galicia and Romania. The new arrivals filled the tailoring shops and increased production by the fruits of industry. New shops opened. In Montreal in 1907 some 20 factories were functioning with some 5000 men and women at work. (...)

The Influence of the Jewish Press on Life
in the U.S.A. and Canada
Israel Medres
Canadian Jewish Chronicle, September 19, 1952

(...) Mr. Hershman felt [in 1902] that if the working man had a chance to read Jewish newspapers regularly, the effect would be more continuous than listening to the occasional speech. The monetary gains which Mr. Hershman could have had from continuing in his factory job or going into another business were not as important as the moral satisfaction of his missionary task of spreading Jewish culture and socialist literature.

On his first day in "business" he received two copies of the *Forvertz*. He kept one for his own use, and sold the other for one cent cash to a Jewish family on St. Felix Street (between Windsor and Mountain Streets) — at that time the heart of the Jewish district with its own *shoykhet* and Jewish milkman; today it is the centre of the Negro community. This first sale was so encouraging that Mr. Hershman decided that newspaper distribution was no longer a hobby, but a real business, deserving all his evenings and week-ends.

At the end of the first year Mr. Hershman moved into his first store on Main Street, at a rental of $5.00 per month. Fearing lest customers would not walk in to buy papers and books, he sublet part of the store for shoe repairs, so that people would have more reason to come in. In spite of his open-door policy, Mr. Hershman still had to go out looking for readers — and he found them among the workers and the peddlers. Unfortunately the working day of twelve or more hours left little time and less energy for reading. The peddler, on the other hand, was out-of-town from Monday to Friday — "out-of-town" being represented by the present area of Ville St. Laurent and Cartierville. St. Jerome was in a different world; further north there wasn't even a road for horse-and-buggy travel.

After 1905, when mass immigration from Russia started, Mr. Hershman was no longer short of customers. Every boatload of immigrants who fled Czarist persecution and army rule, every boatload of Jews seeking their livelihood in a democratic country, every such boatload brought its quota of new readers. Soon after 1905 Mr. Hershman moved to larger quarters, and increased his sale of newspapers, socialist literature, and even handled prayer books and other religious articles.

(...) The term "public relations" was not yet known, but the "deed" of informing the Jewish population of the urgent needs of the day — the "deed" of educating the growing Jewish community about the importance of rescuing the surviving Jews of Europe — this was done effectively and successfully by the Yiddish press.

On a more world-wide scale the Yiddish press began a fight for equal rights wherever there was racial discrimination; it began to clamour for political freedom; the Yiddish press took up the battle cry for a Jewish homeland; it brought to light and fought anti-Semitism; the Yiddish press of the 1918-1920 period was dynamic, vibrant, purposeful and influential.

Another problem which was tackled by the Yiddish press was the one of assimilation. There was a tendency among the wealthier English-speaking Jews to try to restrain the "political" ambitions of the East-Enders. The *Yahudim* even objected to the east-end protests against anti-Semitism. It was the Jewish press that took up the fight of the "Main Street" Jews.

The early 1920s were the most creative years in the field of Jewish journalism and literature. The post-war period brought a new flood of immigrants, amongst whom were many outstanding Jewish writers who sought a haven in Canada and the United States. The leading concert-artists, musicians, authors, and editors of Eastern Europe swelled the ranks of our cultural elite. The status of Jewish journalism was raised considerably. The Jewish newspaper became a living university — a day-to-day text book in philosophy, history, science, Chassidism, Zionism, and other current and important topics. Poetry, dramatizations, and serialized novels found their way into the Yiddish press of the 1920s.

The First Library in Montreal
Hirsch Hershman
Jewish Public Library publication, 1926

As a small child I had great respect for the printed word. My criterion for the greatness and importance of a city was the measure of what the city was known for throughout "the world" by the instrumentality of the printed word; in my case the world was my *shtetl* Starozhivietz. I was very jealous of the boys of the nearby large city of Schatz which had a printery which printed wedding invitations for the area. When we received an invitation the most important was the bottom Hebrew lines "The Herman Beiner Printery of Schatz." So when we later moved to Schatz, my first visit was to "The Herman Beiner Book Printery House," to see with my own eyes how a printery looks.

Another strong impression created by the large city of Schatz was a circle of enlightened readers of newspapers who discussed issues in Polish in the chambers of the synagogue during the Bible reading. I did not quite become acquainted with them; I was too young to be accepted by them. (I met some of them later in Montreal.)

In 1897 I arrived in New York, where I remained until 1902. There I met the Socialist and Labour movement which began to assume a certain form, when Morris Rosenfeld became known through his *My Son*. Abe Cahan lectured, (...) B. Feigenbaum, Philip Krantz, Louis Miller, Morris Winchevsky, Joseph I. Barondess, M. Zmetkin, as well Johan Most and Emma Goldman. Only the privileged ones whose work allowed a measure of time, could go hear these speakers.

The only spiritual material available to a working man was to be read in a newspaper or a pamphlet in the free moments available to him. I remember I once acquired a set of old *Arbeter Tsaytung* in a pushcart, with Abe Cahan's articles entitled "A Quart from a Word" and "From a Proletarian Sermonizer" which had appeared before I reached New York. Some intelligent merchant, aware of the value of these articles, had accumulated sets and done well by distributing them. The set which I had bought made the rounds among my friends; I kept my eyes on them until I lost track of one of those readers. I still miss them.

At the time I became aware of several of my *schatz maskilim* in Montreal, and also that life in Canada was quieter than in New York, almost in the European style (even in tailoring). One does not work as long hours as in New York "sweatshops." I longed for such an environment, and came to Montreal in the summer of 1902.

I met some of the Schatz youths, but my illusions ran dry. Nor did I find the sympathetic environment I anticipated. If only there was a library, a club, a Jewish book store, some public place with a newspaper. The only similar place was a private house on Cadieux[1] near Dorchester[2], the home of the *Tageblat* agent S. Wilensky who had in his home the spiritual articles which Montreal Jews needed: calendars, Grace prayers, printed notes for pregnant women, prayer books for women, High Holiday volumes.

He also had Yiddish books "for women" as he told me at the time. "I keep them for women, for men would not devote their time to such foolishness as storybooks." You could find all that is good of that line, of their famous historical romances of *Catherine the Great* and *The Russian Imperial Court, The Poisoner, Among Cannibals, The Iron Woman,* or *The Child that was Sold.* The last two, Shomer's "best sellers", were particularly popular among "the women." They could be borrowed at two cents a chapter.

But there was no sign of the new literature which had begun to appear in New York, or was being imported from Europe, and when I first asked him about such work as Mendele Mokher Sforim's *The Mare* or *The Wish Finger* or Sholem Aleichem's *People's Library* (*Folksbibliotek*), he did not know their titles, 'What did you say the name was? *The Mare?* a strange title. Never heard of it. Probably a *jargon* story book. I don't have it. I have enough story books for women. I will not bring any new ones.'

It then occurred to me to interest a few men to subscribe some books and papers together from New York. I had in the meantime learned that there were supporters of various movements of socialism here, and thus arose my plan to organize a subscribers' group for literature. Among the first names worthy of note: Joshuah Cars, Moses Goldberg, Meier Eliasoph, Mishkin, Gershovitz, Ellison and L. Shlakman — the last the only surviving activist in the movement. I cannot remember how the group was formed, or the basis of its union, except that in the fall of 1903 I was delegated to New York to acquire literature for our circle, the first Jewish library in Montreal. Why me? Possibly because I had been a New Yorker, or possibly they had already recognized in me a public emissary. I was given a capital of some $20 with instructions to get largely socialist and anarchist literature.

Moses Goldberg recommended some Hebrew literature, but this was quickly rejected. However all agreed on some belles-lettres; some short Shalom Aleichem and Peretz stories; Sholem Asch was mentioned, but "for heaven's sake, more books with a social political tendency."

Arriving in New York I went directly to the office of the *Tsukunft* at 50 Suffolk St. We consulted the manager Harry Netter and some Social Democrats who advised against anarchist literature, but they withdrew their reservations in the light of the Montreal condition.

Within a day or two I was back with a bundle of books which was soon opened in my home at 36 Hermine, near Craig Street. Of our three rooms one was devoted to the library. On a table in the corner stood the whole library: the thin booklets of social political literature, some short items of Peretz, Sholom Aleichem and Abraham Reisen; dramas by Jacob Gordin; some atheistic pamphlets by B. Feigenbaum; *The Cultural History* and *The History of the French Revolution* by Philip Krantz.

The library was open evenings for the librarian, Mrs. Hershman, was occupied all day in helping her "provider," and worked with him in the shop.

Our library was busy evenings; our group consisted of some ten, none of whom failed to come after work, to change a book, to look at the *Forvertz*, to chat or freshen an opinion in a debate.

The sincerest debater was Joshuah Cars, who, when not debating, felt like a fish on dry land. Himself an individualist anarchist Nietzschean, he loved to defend the opposite notion and provoke a discussion and sharpen minds. Since the librarian did not spare the tea, everybody was comfortable in this library until the Passover *Haggadah* hour for the reading of the *shema* prayer.

Time passed and our group did not expand, nor did the literature grow. It had all been perused and had become monotonous. It then occurred to us to open a place to sell the *Forvertz* and other books, brochures, and journals, which, for this purpose was a wooden stall on Main Street and Ontario, rented at five dollars a month. My wife agreed that I continue to work in the shop while she would work in the store, and thus we opened the first Jewish book-store in Montreal where there was no reactionary reading matter.

I recall that when I considered stocking Minikes' *Passover Sheets* I consulted my colleagues whether we should carry so bourgeois a publication, but it was agreed that it published articles by socialist writers and it was admitted. In the store could be found all the books and brochures which we had in our library, and, naturally, the *Forvertz, Tsukunft*, and *Fraye Arbayter Shtime*. The only window was decorated by the papers we had in our library. Our store became famous (or to the contrary) as readers stopped to make out the difficult language of this strange store. Indeed the merchandise of *The Cannibals, The Contractor, The Iron Woman*, and the intelligible texts of the *Mysteries of The Russian Imperial Court*, but now with strange titles like *The History of Culture* and *The History of the French Revolution, The Erfurt Program, The Right to Laziness, The Mare, God, Man and the Devil, The Lie of God, The Lie of the Wedding, The Lie of Religion*, issues of Sholom Aleichem's *People's Library, Der Yid*, the *Forvertz, Tsukunft* and the *Fraye Arbayter Shtime*.

People stood outside our window, looked at the books, discussed them, but none dared enter except our colleagues. Whoever came in decided that something is not right. He could hear expressions such as "The State is the source of human society," "The federative principle," "Private communism" which threw a dread upon all, but everyone kept away.

---

[1] Cadieux Street is now called de Bullion
[2] Dorchester Street is now called René Lévesque Boulevard

35 Years Since the Founding of Congress
Simon Belkin
Keneder Odler, March 10, 1954

We sought to organize Canadian Jews as a national minority with the same rights as other groups in the country. The older settlers rejected the plan, but we were young, resolute and optimistic. We saw the organization of Jews in each country as part of a world-wide national unity. This united world can ensure our national unity in the diaspora, and international respect, with Canada as a state of nationalities where the English and the French enjoy equal rights — and the Ukrainians and the Poles in western Canada — in regard to language, cultural autonomy and national organization; national rights for Canadian Jews, we felt, are not against the constitution.

Some felt that these rights will be limited to school rights. Yehudah Kaufman and Dr. C. Zhitlowsky participated in a strategy meeting of delegates at the Congress sessions; this group decided not to press the issue at the formal session. They reasoned that a permanent congress would eventually come to deal with this question. It would suffice for the present to work for cultural autonomy.

We have always felt that the work in the Congress and for the Congress constitute a program of national significance in that the Canadian community is the best organized group among the exiles.

Light Pieces

Frontispiece of the *Pinkhas* (synagogue record book) maintained by
Yehiel Herman between 1906 and 1952, He was the *shames* of
Tifereth Jerusalem or Rossland synagogue in the Papineau district
of Montreal. The congregation is now located in Hampstead, Quebec.
*Courtesy of Congregation Tifereth Beth David Jerusalem
and the Jewish Public Library.*

The *Keneder Odler*, with its almost entirely immigrant readership, could not approach everyday life in Montreal solely as a ceaseless struggle for justice and human dignity or an ideological battle against the exploitation of the toiling masses in the garment factories of St. Lawrence Boulevard. The readership of the paper also consisted of simple people recently torn from the comforting and familiar setting of the *shtetl*, who enjoyed reading lighter pieces in the vein of the great Eastern European Yiddish writers such as Sholom Aleichem and I.L. Peretz. The authors of these humorous chronicles, who were often from elsewhere, made fun of the Jews both in Montreal and in the rest of the diaspora. They allow us today to see these immigrants and their foibles from a point of view different from their own. This type of writing was such a success that the owner of the *Keneder Odler* even published a paper entirely devoted to humour, called *Der Hamer* (The Hammer), for a few years during the period that interests us.

Four pieces clearly stand out among the humorous writing published in the early years of the century in the *Keneder Odler*; all of them are about the Jews of the Papineau district. Very few people today remember that the Jewish community of Montreal before World War I had a little satellite group located around Papineau Street, in an area that was then semi-rural. Around 1914, this partly Yiddish-speaking area, bounded on the west by Garnier Street, on the east by Chabot Street, and on the north by Bélanger Street, contained at most 225 Jewish families. There were two synagogues, including the justly famous Tifereth Jerusalem, which left to posterity a *pinkhas* [record book] containing unique historical material, as well as a free loan association, a mutual insurance company, and a school for young children. Interestingly, the Papineau district, which was developed by the Ross realty company, was known as Rossland, a name that is very close phonetically to *Rusland,* the Yiddish name for Russia, the country of origin of the majority of the Montreal Jews.

At the beginning of the century, the Jewish residents of Papineau were exceptional in more than one way in the Montreal context. Whereas the vast majority of the Yiddish-speaking population at the time were crowded into the overpopulated district near the port and worked in garment factories or small businesses where sanitary conditions were very difficult, those in Papineau lived in a green environment, often worked as small craftsmen, and in many cases owned modest homes. In this district they could even keep domestic animals. They could fraternize with their non-Jewish neighbours and live side-by-side with French-Canadian religious institutions without difficulty. These exceptional social and cultural characteristics gave rise in the Montreal Jewish imagination of the time to a perception of Papineau as a land of plenty literally on the margins of Jewish society, where all the rules of Jewish life were turned upside down.

One Must Have Luck
Reuben Brainin
Presumed to be *Keneder Odler*, December 18, 1908

Luck is essential! Without it you might as well lie down and cry to the Lord, without Him there is no success.

I have done every possible thing in my life, but poverty pursues me (may this not happen to you), like a brother in the flesh who watches over me incessantly.

You may possibly think, God forbid, that I am of no significance, a foundling on the street or descended from plain people. *Feh*, nothing of the sort. I do not like to boast. Fine family, they say, is a matter for cemeteries. But I tell you straight out that I am kneaded only from rabbis. I am a grandchild of the composer of "Him who assists the poor" and a great-grandchild of the author of "The Supporter of the Best." And do you know who my grandmother was?

But what is the value of all this? I'll give you a blown out egg for my genealogy. In this land everybody is an esquire: everybody tells wonder tales of his genealogy. But who believes us or considers us? We are all beggars here, paupers. Is this not true? The family chart keeps you neither cold nor warm.

But you think I am ignorant or not very clever, an ordinary man, and that is why I am a peddler. Excuse me, Uncle, but you are wrong. But it makes no difference if you do not believe me. I would not become Rothschild if you did believe me. But since we are chatting, I thought I would tell you.

For no reason I am telling you I know the Talmud thoroughly, not to speak of Maimonides, and you do not know philosophy and all its questionings and refinements. I should be so lucky as I am — thanks to the Lord — a bit of a questioner and one of the enlightened. My Hebrew is still sugar sweet. But who needs it here? Here all is cash, ringing cash. Without that you are nothing, a nothing of nothing.

You might think I am lazy: that is why I am of ill luck. But where have I not yet been? At all the world's ends; America in all its lengths and breadth. But wherever I came my poverty was with me. We are a couple like other couples.

Some people were fortunate. Servants become masters; craftsmen became manufacturers. But I (...) You cannot help me, nor do I want your help. Can a man help another man? I am only saying the Creator of the universe has punished me, so how anyone can ask Him questions, why did He pick on me? Am I such a *tzadik*? I am no saint, for how can you be a saint when your world is managed upside down? My troubles have turned me into an agnostic. I see clearly that neither Torah learning nor wisdom, neither energy nor piety — nothing helps in the absence of luck. And, uncle, you might think that I have travelled only through America? I have searched for luck in England. Should I list the trying at everything, the skills and trades I worked at? But why fill your head when it has its own troubles? But who does not have his own?

I only want you not to believe I am lazy. When I saw that there was no slice of bread for me in England, I jumped to Paris. Does a lazy man do this? These Frenchmen are nice enough people and Paris is a free city, but they do not know English and I have no French.

In short, I wandered over the streets and boulevards of Paris and among the Jews there. But nothing helps when there is no luck in Paris. Things were so bad in Paris that I had considered putting an end to all my troubles and jumping into the Seine, and "adieu." But as it is said, you live perforce.

If you ask me why I live and what I expect from living, I will answer — nothing but troubles greater than the last ones. But strangely when I was about to jump into the Seine, something kept me back. There must be a spring in the life machine that does not permit you to end life suddenly before the time has come.

You laugh at my questionings. I don't mind. Let a Jew enjoy himself. I only mention that the life that is in us is a sort of electricity in a hidden little machine and if the wheels need to turn they cannot be stopped perforce. Isn't it so? For it is a well known fact that when you live, you want to eat. And I tell you, uncle, that eating is a nasty thing, that when you want to eat, you must find bread. And when I did not find my piece of bread in Paris — and I needed so little — and I did not want to starve or to jump into the Seine, so what did I do? I packed myself off to Germany. That is a long and sad story. *Feh*, it is an ugly thing to be a poor man (...).

I tried to earn something in Germany, but they simply sent me out. All sorts of arguments did not help. I was given a ticket to the border. You are a bit of a sensible person, so you will understand what happened at the Russian-Polish border. I had been born there and spent my youth there and did not want to go back there. What will I do there? Explore the walls, knock on doors for alms, where everybody eats everybody. Some country, Poland! But a Jew has no choice. When he is told to go, he must go where his eyes direct him as where he is pushed.

So in the middle of the night I left Germany — some country, Germany, long may it burn, please the Creator of the universe! I tell you, Uncle, the Germans are wild animals, torturers of Jews. Please try to be a saint and not become an agnostic.

You tell me, we the Jews, the chosen people, must wander as aliens, eternally, and the Germans, incontestable [lit.: eighteen dimensional] pigs, eaters of forbidden sausages, cannibals, should ride on all and play such a part in the world.

But all questionings aside, I had to take my prayer shawl and my phylacteries, some old books and my feet on my shoulders — and off, where? to Belgium. If I had not been there before, so you find me here too.

So here I am in Antwerp, as you see, some two years; I live and I trade and no one bothers me. The Belgians are dear gentle people, love to live and let live, the police look and are silent, and our brethren, the sons of Israel, mostly Polish Jews, are good people who do not hate a poor man. They wanted to turn me into a diamond merchant, a traveller. They wanted to give me a package of diamonds to peddle them in the cafés where merchants sit and do business. Very many live from this trade, and some are well-to-do.

So what does mine do? I repeat 'no,' even though I am honoured to be considered as an honest man; they trust me with a package of merchandise that I pray that you and I may possess its true value. But I repeat 'no.' I would not be a diamond dealer, I would not abet a sin, you understand? Some do-nothing wants to present some female a diamond to influence her to a sin. Do you hear? I need to be a broker to the dead? May he never live to see the day. This is no business for me.

I began dealing with other objects — prayer books, hooks, buttons, knives, matches, shoe laces, etc. Useful things that both gentiles and Jews need. Buy, Uncle, I will not overcharge you. I am not forcing you to buy. The Blessed God will send me other customers. But I do need luck. You want to know about my children? That is quite another story. But please buy something. I haven't made a sale today. I do need luck.

An Interview with the *Shul Shames*
Isaac Yampolsky
Keneder Odler, December 19, 1913

When I entered before the first assembly for the morning prayer he was standing, broom in hand, looking at a corner near the Sacred Ark at a small pile of dirt covered with spider webs.

Clearly he was wondering whether he should leave it or wait for the eve of Passover. I did not want to disturb his thoughts, and stood to one side and devoted a few minutes to quiet examination.

He was an interesting figure, with a round head and large round hat. Only the nose (...) gave assurance of his belonging to the Semitic race. His beard had begun to grow only with age, his cheeks were naked, eyes small, deep, reddish at the brows, clearly a deep thinker.

When he saw me he gave me his friendly '*Shalom Aleichem.* You are observing the anniversary of a loss?'

'No', I said, 'my parents are with us, may they live long.' He said, 'Do you need phylacteries, a prayer shawl?'

'No, not that either. I have already prayed this morning.' (...) He said, 'In that case, what are you doing in *shul*?'

I said, 'I came to ask whether you would be kind enough to let me interview you as you see I am a newspaper reporter.'

'If it is for the public good,' he smiled, 'why not?'

We sat on a narrow bench near the door, at a long table. He put the broom on the table, took out the snuff box and took a sniff of tobacco. I took out a Federal Tobacco cigarette and asked permission to light up. 'Certainly. Here we smoke, we eat, we drink whiskey, we sleep. Why not? Do you think we are German?

'(...) I am ready,' said the *shames* (...), 'but I would ask you to convey each word. For I have heard say that your gang of reporters are, you will excuse me, great liars. They write the opposite of what we tell them and think up stories that never happened.'

'I swear by the sanctity of this holy place' (I told him); I swear by the sanctity of our writers and by the pictures of our circumcisers, cantors and by the husbands who have disappeared that I will not alter a word which you will tell me. With one exception. Instead of writing that you are a sexton I will write that it is the chief rabbi that I have interviewed. Would you consider it an offence?'

'God forbid. Who speaks of offence in America? I am only doing this to render a service. But let us begin, for as you know this is the eve of *Hanuka* and I am somewhat busy.'

'It is about *Hanuka* that I wish to speak to you. (...) Have you prepared a stock of *Hanuka* candles?'

'Truth to tell, I did not put up a big stock because even my best members take advantage of the Christmas candles from the church for their *Hanuka menorahs*.'

'Is it true, as the papers write, that you are going on strike?' I asked him.

'It is nearly true,' he said.

'But you are not sure?' I asked.

'I am sure that our cantor will not scab to take over the *shames* job. At the least he will sympathize with me, but I am not at all sure of my rabbi.'

'How come the cantor sympathizes with the *shames*?' I asked, amazed.

'Because I can read the Hebrew and I can sing better than him, so he is afraid that I may become the cantor.'

'I don't understand.' I asked, 'why are you afraid of the rabbi?'

'You can play around with our rabbi?'

'When,' I asked, 'will you know?'

'When an organizer will come around.'

'You belong to a union?' I asked.

'To the Union of *Shamosim*, the biggest in the country.'

'Why,' I asked, 'have you never told our paper that your *shamossim* Union organizer is coming?'

'I can't answer that one.'

'Does that mean that you will not strike this year?'

'That depends on this *Hanuka* season. If there will not be a strong market for festival candles, we will call out all the *shamosim* from all the synagogues and say 'Stop!' until they meet our demands.'

'Do you have strong perspectives for a demand for *Hanuka* candles?'

'And how! You know that the Zionist Convention has been called for *Hanuka*. Can you imagine how many candles will be demanded by the delegates?'

'No.' I asked, 'What happens if the Zionists will be satisfied with Christian Christmas candles?'

'That is when we will go out in a real strike.' (...)

'What are your demands for weekday prayer hours?'

'We will demand that the rabbi and cantor should also attend weekday prayers, evenings and mornings. Why should only we proletarian *shamosim* pray? Secondly, we ask that all Jews should buy their candles from us rather than get Christian candles. We work hard to make candles and we light candles in our sacred synagogues, and they go out and get Christian candles! Shame on them, the loiterers, back to your own houses of worship!'

He grabbed the broom and ran off. I pushed my cap on my head firmly and left the synagogue for the editorial office.

A Little About *Batlones*
Shayele Veverekes
Der Veg, February 11, 1916

Sayeth[1] Rabbi Dr. Coralnick, 'Jews are *batlanim.*'

From whence do we know this? Never mind from whence. We know this all right. We have evidence! Take, for instance, doctors; not medical men, God forbid, but greater than these doctors, professors, and most of them are *batlanim.* Today where are the schoolmen, the *yeshivah* students, the famed Ten *Batlanim* (upon whom the entire universe stands) and then the ordinary *batlanim*?

"The matter having reached this far," [as the sages put it[2]], he asks a *kashe*: why do we not make a picture of him? Of the *batlan*, that is, it is most important for us to fix him artistically for the ages.

In his conclusion of the tractate he lets out a fiery thought: Herzl was a practical man and the Ussishkin was a *batlan*, and the conflict between streams in Zionism is nothing more than *batlones*.

"Along came Tzivion[3]" [to dismiss the question once and for all.] He is certain that there are *goyim* who are *batlanim* and, as Jews assimilate, they also become *batlanim*.

I want to bring two examples and to ask the two great authorities in this field of *batlones*, where does the *batlan* begin and where does the practical man end?

These days I passed by a monastery and saw two monks skating in a fenced-in area, playing "the hockey match."[4] I became very upset: is it possible? How can monks, who make a living from *batlones,* who hold the patent for *batlanut* and a monopoly on this — how does life bring them to this contradiction? Men who distance themselves from the world and seek to sanctify themselves, to create a new life, free and pure of earthly pleasures, of bodily excesses, publicly go about to practice the opposite? (...)

And again several days ago two men came to our editorial office, not "labourers," God forbid, or "intellectuals," but businessmen, very practical people indeed.

They had gone out for supper and began to converse as usual, and an argument arose: one said it is certain that rocks grow, as he had heard; and the second became excited and screamed that he knows in all certainty that it is not so. He heard that there is a science which proves precisely the opposite.

So they both came to the editor for a clear answer as to which of them is correct. They put everything aside, forgot their supper for which they usually have a firm appetite, forgot their own business and went off investigating and debating.

You may say that they are *batlanim*; so the question arises; if *batlones* was learned from the *goyim*, where are there such *batlanim* among the *goyim*?

No, Mr. Tzivion, our *batlanim* are "original natives", not copies.

And I say that we have reason to be happy that we have so many *batlanim*. We have long been taught that *batlanim* create our history; they have given us our survival. As an exile people it is our good fortune to have *batlanim*.

You would rid yourself of them, and we ask you how can this be done? You cannot send all the *batlanim* to take courses at the *Forvertz* nor is it necessary.

As to Coralnick wanting to have the *batlanim* artistically perpetuated, we will ask him, is it necessary?

The more articles we have à la "In distant Canada," "The *batlan*, and the Jewish Congress," the sooner we will have an eternal monument to the typical *batlan* of our time.

---

[1] In original "Amar" (Aramaic form of the verb, alluding to Talmudic style)
[2] The Aramaic phrases in this paragraph and the next are indicated with "double quote" marks.
[3] This in the nom-de-plume of B. Hoffman
[4] "The hockey match" was in quotes in the original, and in English, as were other phrases in quotes later in the text.

A Walk in Papineau
B.J. Goldstein (under the name of Reb Boruchel)
Keneder Odler, June 5th and 19th, 1910

[I had long intended to go to Papineau,] but it is a long and complicated trip, with several cars constantly changing direction. [But] the hope never died in me to go to the legendary Papineau. The very 'niou' ending of the name was exciting. At home when they added a 'niou' to a person's name it indicated that he was a special person; if he hits you in the face you will see stars and your grandmother in her grave (...)[1]

The wondrous tales they tell of Papineau: of the goats that live in trees there, that [the stranger will not touch money on the street, but nails and boards must be kept in safes.] You need to post a detachment of soldiers to guard them, and even then you are not secure.

Another spoke of Papineau as a Jewish realm, and children born there had to be taken to the city to see a French Canadian or an Irishman. But a third witness testified that there are more French than Jews there and that their rascals get into fights with our Jews on the street when they find weaklings. A bluffer told me that there are two moons to be seen every night in Papineau, and that the sky is so low that people must walk bent over. (...) Another told me that Jews never quarrel there, and that trees are always red with black leaves.

I advise my readers to go to Papineau to drink milk there, eat *latkes*, and they will be my friends for life.

'How do you like our Papineau? Come on in and see it from the inside.' He brought me to his poultry, his garden where all that is good grows luxuriantly, and explained every variety; 'these are berries, and these are vines, genuine grapes, only the chickens pulled them down; we planted onions here and potatoes.'

'They have an evil decree here; we are not allowed to work Sundays. If you drive a nail in on that day, you can be martyred, and fined $20, that thief America, not even a single nail. So it took us longer; within the week you will find a fortress here,' as he shows me where the bedroom will be, where the front room and where the kitchen.

Another resident complained, 'We met fifteen times and decided to put up a small synagogue. A community must have a sacred place where they can have something of a *minyan*, where we can quarrel and sometimes even slap around a bit.' They have forgotten that they have laid a foundation, that they have already invested some $150, and now they are begging outside

Papineau. One Mr. Lazar longs for a synagogue of his own where he could pour his heart out in prayer for a good year, pour his heart out to the Creator of the Universe and, if necessary, poke the *parnas* in his ribs because he injects some Torah teachings without authority. Yet I had to promise him to do something to realize his project.

I dropped into the library, a fine black case with a window in the centre with the markings of some store. The librarian was polishing the glass and the doors. There are all sorts of works for sale here, on dentistry and on mandolin playing, a hat with a feather, pyjamas without buttons, books on philosophy, pictures of couples looking at each other after declaring love; and if you need a stovepipe hat or a pair of glasses... In short, if you walk in naked, you can emerge a regular Yankee with a book under your arm. Which is why it is called the Library.

Another told me, 'You know we also have congregations, societies and parties whose meetings last deep into the night, sometimes till the cocks crow. Chickens are numerous in Papineau and each can raise the dead from their slumber. So you can imagine all the roosters of Papineau beginning to compete and to force the meetings to come to an end.'

A congregation wrote a member who owed one dollar: 'By order of the president, it was decided to inform you by registered mail that if you do not come to settle the account, the matter will be turned over to a lawyer. We ask you to come and pay and to save the considerable expense.'

Such letters are not proper for congregations who will soon learn better, for some members may not always be able to pay their dues.

Generally *les Papineau* live in harmony. On Sundays they welcome visitors from the city. Some days a thousand come and — it is well that they do not hear this — they often develop a strange appetite and they dispose of all that has been prepared and grind it all up. Their hosts encourage them. 'Eat, take some more,' advice that is followed energetically. I hope no one comes to my home.

I tell you, fine people, these Papineaus.

---

[1] Yiddish-speaking immigrants had the habit of pronouncing Papineau as "Papiniou", which is a measure of their attachment to this neighbourhood, since it also means "little father" in Russian.

Papineau Neighbourhood

B.J. Goldstein (under the name of Reb Boruchel)
Keneder Odler, June 10, 1910

As I have once told you, the people of Papineau are honest people. Even the conductors who take you there are honest. The first one did not accept fare from me. The second thought long about the wisdom of the astronomers and asked for double fare. The third considered the transfers on all sides, shook his head, and returned them to me with a smile. 'I don't know whether the transfers are *kosher* or *treyf*, but there is no doubt that you are a nice man.' And with the fourth, the car went very slowly so that I could read all the signs and count the panes in every window. And soon we were in Papineau.

There is a great green wooded place, like a field, with tall trees, with branches chopped so that they appear like slim ladies in tight fitting suits without hips. The trees with the cut-off branches and the rubbed bark stand in fear when they see strangers, as they anticipate axes in the hand. Among these trees there are black boxes which make one shiver, reminding me of graves with letters. But these are homes where people live, eat, drink and sleep.

But the car stopped and I entered into the home of a young man in a red brick house, recently erected, with large mirrors, with a chopped down tree in the courtyard at the corner, looking down with sympathy at a reduced Jewish citizen.

The young man with glasses, without a jacket, and a cheerful, hospitable smile, led me to where a number of cows and a Christian wearing a cap on the side served us with a glass of warm milk. We then helped carry out the fine table and the fine benches under the fine sky. We took off the fine jackets and began to drink the aromatic tea and began to eat the dairy *latkes* and sipped the red wine and enjoyed it no end.

From the distance we could also see guests at other tables under the open sky, with samovars, some with tea kettles, the sky indifferent to the frogs at concert. The area was still, with a distant hum. It seemed far from the city, people, and noise, (...) seldom a distant laughter from one of the tables. No fire anywhere in sight except the ice cream parlour where I could swear shines an electric lamp.

I cannot speak for others, but I had no desire to go home. I could stay here all night under the open sky, like the young man sleeping near us so pleasantly, presenting us a concert with his nose. Yes, I would lie down here, but now a rain is coming down, and the sky is no longer friendly, and we had to go home.

But before concluding I must inform you that I visited the library, I saw the synagogue, spoke to some Papineau residents. But I propose to delay this for a few days later, God willing, if He grants me the good life. I shall tell you all at length. For the present I would notify that if you wish to see all these antiques, you should hasten the more, for soon they will pack the black boxes and the white nails, and will put up fine homes with red bricks, and you will see nothing.

Take my advice, and make it sooner.

Papineau District
E. Boulay
Keneder Odler, November 28, 1911

Recently I took the Amherst street car, transferred at St. Jean de Berchmans up Papineau Road where, I knew, there was an important Jewish settlement.

Some told me the area was called St. Jean de Berchmans, others Rossland, but I think it is generally known as Rosemont.

Clearly there are many Jews there; more than 200 families set up their homes in this new centre of activity. (...) Their families are not small, [no different from our French Canadian families.] Their children play happily near their poor, small homes; not exactly palaces, but the children are satisfied.

These Jews have opened groceries and other small stores, and new buildings have sprouted nearby honouring the Jewish spirit of enterprise and exemplary economy.

Most of them arrived here without money, but they managed to acquire land by virtue of their patience and energy, and to set up their homes; some of them are still being built. Wilder, the owner of the furniture store, was one of the thirty-four pioneers of Rosemont.

I would wish my French Canadians followed their example in enterprise.

It leads us to speculate whether this race is truly indestructible. It might well have sunk under the weight of persecution during centuries.

The Jews of Rosemont, but a few miles from the city, can in fact live the life of the village. Many of their homes may not have been built artistically;

the interior of others many not be complete, but they all feel at home. The residents are nearly all property owners; they are attached to their nests.

They act as in families, unceremoniously, in accordance with custom, with common openness and sympathy. There is no polish here. The Jewish ladies of Rosemont do not hesitate to go to the well for water. (...) They live amicably with their Christian neighbours. There is a measure of mistrust because they do not know each other well. But peace will reign if our anti-Semitic sectarians will not plant their poison here.

The Catholics have a church and a school here, and the Jews have a fine synagogue and are building another.

I only regret that I cannot speak to them in the language of their ancestors. I would wish to hear the secret of their success in their mother tongue, but with my poor English I could at best feel the sense of their heart.

Papineau Road
Dr. Ezekiel Wortsman
Keneder Odler, November 13, 1910

We can console all who bewail the decline of Jewish life in exile.

Widely spread Judaism may not be aware of the news, so we consider it our duty to announce that they may rejoice that Papineau Road has two Jewish congregations; Papineau Road is building two synagogues for prayer. It will have two cantors, two presidents and two sets of "sacred vessels," religious functionaries.

Your geographical learning may not reach so far, nor are you aware of this Jewish kingdom; there may be other Jewish kingdoms outside your ken. So learn and enjoy learning.

Papineau Road is a suburb of Montreal, the capital. It has no running water, sewers, light, no health or life. But it has two communities of Jews, mainly poor and depressed, most of them labourers and peddlers. It has no Talmud Torah, and many children grow up without a trace of Jewish learning. Yet this kingdom already has two communities with the resounding titles, *Chaverim Kol Israel* ('All Israel are Comrades,') and the *Tifereth Jerusalem* ('Glory of Jerusalem').

We report on two congregations already, but before writing this editorial this settlement may acquire a third, possibly the 'Extension of the Berdichev Congregation,' or a fourth, the 'Congregation of all Israel are Enemies,' and before this is printed Papineau may have a fifth, the 'Congregation of the Observers of Tuesdays', and so on.

For Papineau already has two hundred Jews and, with our growing population we might acquire another five Jews, and if Mr. A is president and Mr. B is *gabay*, and Mr. C is treasurer are D and E, and etc., lesser persons?

All this is no joke, for we lack words for this form of Jewishness. We had believed that when Jews will leave the lands where they had been deprived of civil and human rights, where they had been confined to ghetto politics; when these Jews came to these free lands, where they can enjoy all freedoms, they will rise above the village pettiness, to a vivid sense of life, and a further and more interesting range. Yet it appears that they have transplanted the quarrels of Eishishock and are bringing our entire city to shame for reasons of vanity and parish pump dissidence.

"Leaders" of one congregation on Papineau Road come to us to malign the members of the other; then those from the latter visit us to tell all that is evil about the first.

Who needs two synagogues in the kingdom of Papineau? We may accept that they need a chapel there for undisturbed prayer; but why two, to waste money and energy and power for victory, when one is too many? Yes, power, a curse that is not mentioned in the Bible. Everybody seeks to teach the other a lesson, to prove his strength.

Judaism does not interest either party in Papineau any more than the snows of yesteryear. If it were otherwise, they would first put up a class for children where they would teach a word of Yiddish, about our great past; they would set up a club where they could read a paper after work, discuss communal affairs. Instead they multiply synagogues to quarrel about cantors and chicken killers (*shokhtim*). Is this how Judaism blossoms in Canada?

Papineau Synagogue
Hirsch Wolofsky (under the name of Yankel Shmid)
Keneder Odler, November 27, 1910

If you put a copy of the *Odler* between them, you could not spread it out. (...) They have no money, (...) but they bought two lots at $500, and the members are busy cutting boards and banging nails as smoke arises, so that in short order we will have a synagogue.

But matters cannot rest so easily; last Sunday Rabbi H. Cohen and other Montreal dignitaries were called out to celebrate the initiation of the construction of the 'All Israel are Comrades' (*Chaverim Kol Israel*) Congregation.

I'll tell you how we get there. You take a street car and change to another car, then to a smaller car, then to the large car, where a smaller car awaits you with the sign, 'To Jerusalem'; the sign is not yet made, but it should be; it will take you to Papineau.

Let me tell you my view of our Papineau comradeship: Papineau is growing, and there will be as much gold as there is mud there now, and a third congregation will arise. The 'Searchers for Peace Congregation,' exactly between the two, and the Searchers will search for peace until they break the walls to the two others and will rename the new structure the 'Great Chapel of Papineau,' and to appease the two synagogues, the new congregation will be called 'Tifereth Jerusalem Chaverim Kol Israel, the Searchers for Peace, and the Great Chapel of Papineau.'

I would therefore advise the candidates for the presidency of the large synagogue (and who does not want to be a candidate?) to memorize its name. For is it appropriate for a president to open a meeting as he stutters at pronouncing its name?

Fiction

Israel Orenstein and his family and chauffeur, Roberval, Quebec, 1917.
Canadian Jewish Congress National Archives.

ALMOST ALL THE JOURNALISTS of the *Keneder Odler* had literary aspirations at some time in their careers. The figure of the writer was highly respected in the Yiddish-speaking world, even in an environment as unrefined as Montreal in the early twentieth century, and writers and intellectuals personified the great leap forward of Jewish culture toward modernity and emancipation. Yiddish poets, playwrights, non-fiction writers, and men of letters in general won admiration — and often notoriety — among the Eastern European Jewish masses. In this context it is not surprising that aspiring literary writers who wanted to reach a broad public flocked to the *Keneder Odler* from the outset. In addition, Wolofsky's newspaper was for a long time the only one in Canada with the resources and the diversified readership to be able to publish non-journalistic writing.

Thus the *Keneder Odler* for several decades, if not for the whole Yiddish literary period, served as an incubator for the new talent that emerged on the Montreal scene. Practically all the writers who started out in the city before 1945 owed their careers in some way to the patronage of the paper. Some, whose talent was greater or who were able to adapt more easily to the demands of journalism, even found permanent jobs there or were given regular columns that brought them a minimum income. However, very few literary writers began their careers in Montreal before World War I, and most of the texts David Rome left us — with the possible exception of those by Hirsch Hershman — were written by individuals who had arrived in the city already educated and in full control of their craft.

Before 1914, the *Keneder Odler* was a publication whose literary models and themes were still drawn from Eastern Europe. The majority of works cited by David Rome in this section are set in the Eastern European Yiddish world or at least express perceptions very close to that universe. However, unlike Brainin, Goldstein, or Yampolsky, Hershman published a piece in the *Odler* set in a rural Quebec context in which the Jews were a tiny minority; it was entitled "A Quebec Story." Although we do not know the exact date of this story and cannot even be absolutely certain that it was published in the *Keneder Odler*, there is no doubt as to its significance. It marks the emergence of a Yiddish literary sensibility characteristic of Quebec — a sensibility that was to blossom between the two world wars, in the poetry of Jacob Isaac Segal, Noach Isaac Gotlieb, and Ida Maze.

A Jewish Wife
Reuben Brainin[1]
Keneder Adler, March 27, 1913

Rachel's husband was a great Talmudic scholar but she had no notion of what his greatness consisted. She knew only that he never looked into her face and did not speak to her much.

Four renowned men endowed him with the title of *Gaon*, but she did not know the meaning of the word. All she knew was that he was buried in his tomes day and night. She had not the faintest notion of what he was seeking there and whether he had found it there, why these men praised him or why his friends were so jealous of her.

Rachel knew that she was married to her husband according to the law of Moses and Israel. But she did not know the morals of their law, nor why Moses and Israel imposed such chains upon her hands. She was faithful to her husband without any idea of what this faithfulness meant or what else could be. She knew that she was the mother of a three-year-old whom she loved with heart and soul, but she did not know that she was beautiful. When her child became sick, the Christian doctor whom she called whispered it into her ear for the first time. Nor did she know why the doctor whispered this to her. She knew only that she became red with shame, but it had been pleasant to hear it.

After the child recovered the doctor no longer visited her house. She almost regretted that he was well again and that she therefore had no further need of him; his words were so loving, so new.

Sometimes she felt unwell and possibly needed his assistance herself and wanted to send for him, but she controlled her melancholy spirit. She was missing his deep, black eyes and pale face and did not know what this yearning meant.

She felt guilty for having listened to his compliments and for not having driven him from her house — a criminal and a woman who had sinned. She defended herself with thoughts of her sick child, but deeply she knew that she listened to his words because they had captured her heart and enchanted her soul; she was a fearful sinner for listening to such words from a strange man, a Christian at that. She did not look her husband or her parents in the eyes. Her sins seemed etched upon her face.

Her husband felt nothing, and her parents did not sense any sin in her. Yet she suffered a deep change: a hidden fear and a secret longing; her blood which had always been in repose, seemed to be constantly restless; her heart, ever still like a spring, had become a stormy sea.

Had she by enchantment lost her sanity or had she lost it long ago? She did not know.

She was sitting quietly but her eyes wandered from side to side. She walked to the window, bent her ear to the door.

It opened and he entered. A shudder ran through her whole body. Her whole being became a question mark.

'All are well here; what does *mein Herr* want?'

'I am not only a doctor, but also a patient. Also a poet in search of beauty which is my god, and the personification of beauty. You are my god and I kneel before you.'

'Sir, you are truly sick'

'I am ill and you can cure me.'

'I don't understand what *mein Herr* means.'

'For that reason, I am a poet.'

'A poet? What is such a poet?'

(...) 'I search and you are the flower. That is why I came in the midst of the thorns. You are not a fading flower; you have not yet bloomed, you have not yet sucked the sweetness of the sun's rays. (...) You do not yet know of love, of life although you are yourself the well of life and of love.'

'I am a Jewish daughter, a sick woman, ill of soul, a stranger to life. (...) I have a child and have become old even when I was young.' (...)

'I will restore your youth which you have never enjoyed.

Youth never returns. What was is no longer. Indeed, what was will never be again. But you can become another, a nobler creature, more loving, more developed and more perfect — if you so wish.'

(...) She lowered her eyes, but his eyes were fixed on her and on her pale face, his fingers caressed her hand.

(...) 'Your hand is so gentle, delicate, telling of a secret life not yet lived, not yet satisfied, yearning, secrets which no one has felt.

'I have long ago given my hand to a man.'

'But not your heart. (...) Tell me, you rose of the deepest valley, have you the courage to be mine, to make me yours, so we can fly to the highest peaks of life, love and happiness?'

'I can never be yours. It cannot be. I was born in the valley and shall die here.'

'You were born in the vale, but you are the daughter of the high peaks. You are a sublime song, a distant yearning.'

'These are sublime words, but I am a simple Jewish daughter, the mother of a child and the slave of life. I have no wings, for they have been clipped'.

'I want nothing from you; only to return to you your beauty, purity and the nobility which dwells in you unbeknownst. (...) If you do not feel your soul, I sense its depths. I wish to resolve all your riddles.' (...)

A baby cried in the adjoining room. Rachel rose 'I was born a Jewish woman and I will die a Jewish woman. This is my answer to you. My child is crying'.

The doctor walked away. No one knew of his coming or of his going. No one saw her tears.

----

[1] Originally written by Brainin in Hebrew – the subtitle says "translated from Hebrew."

A Penny
B.J. Goldstein
Keneder Odler, November 1, 1908

It is already the third day that it has been torturing him.

And he is friendless in his new home. Alien and cold is everything here (...) alien and cold he is nearly himself to his ideal which had brought him here to this vast new world (...) to all those with whom he slowly shared the slices of bread which he had had. And now he had nothing (...)

And the days drag slowly, empty (...)

He had turned the newspaper over many times, looked over the advertisements, but the hunger would not be forgotten.

"Already the third hunger-day!"

There in the park, in a corner near the iron fence, the aged woman is calling out her wares:

'A penny for a roll! A penny!'

The odour sneaks out to him, warm, promising, pleasant.

In seriousness (...), he is becoming dizzy from the reading. He shakes the paper in front of him but he sees nothing, the paper waves in front of him, the lines weaving inside each other into one blot, making his eyes dizzy, and making his head and his brain spin.

His mouth is dry. A dry white skin covers his lips (...) His life has become centred in a corner within him. It will soon spring forth and will leave him on the bench, faint, dead.

"The third hunger-day."

His exploring fingers found his vest pocket and there (...)

He trembled to life.

A coin, a Russian *kopeck*.

Lazily, slowly he rose from his bench, his legs confused, he crept to the peddler of the rolls.

The aroma of her baked goods made his head reel. (...)

He grabbed a roll and quickly and feverishly sank his teeth in it (...) quickly and feverishly he cast the coin into the basket as quickly and feverishly he went off into another corner.

The old woman fished the coin out from amid the rolls.

'May he choke, the thief! A Russian *kopeck*, the thief.'

Yankele the Insane
I. Yampolsky
Presumed to be in *Keneder Odler*, no date.

Yankele was a happy beggar. He constantly argued with the wealthy, he never feared them, had no respect for them, and called on a substantial portion of impertinence. Because these are qualities appropriate to the wealthy, Yankele was nominated "Insane".

It did appear as if all was not right in his head, for he seems to have had no sense of the difference between the rich and the poor; more correctly, he did not feel poor. Instead he considered himself a poor millionaire, and all his acts, demands and conduct were those of a wealthy man.

He never begged for alms; rather he demanded, and no one ever refused him, for his very demand evoked a certain respect.

He would eat all week in cheap rooming houses, but he loved to eat well on the Sabbath; as he would say, at his own table at home. This home was at the tables of the several leading citizens of the community to whom he would write on Wednesdays or Thursdays, 'Tell your spouse to expect me for the

Sabbath;' and the lady expected him richly, she knew that Yankele might well bring a guest with him and tell the hostess to give his guest a goodly portion of his plate.

More than once Yankele would be angry at his host if the fish or the sweet vegetables were not to his taste. 'You are always at home, and you do nothing. Can you not attend and make certain that the hostess cook better?'

The man of the house enjoys his own generosity richly; the children laugh and Yankele leans back on his padded chair in the face of his host and expatiates seriously, 'If I were rich and you the poor man, I would take care of you better'.

The host enjoys himself and asks Yankele, 'So why are you not the rich man?'

Yankele responds seriously, 'Because I cannot be a pig, as I see that the rich are the worst people in the world. It is good that they are so few, and the others are flocks of cattle, stupid, tramps who only know to work like donkeys and to eat like horses and to quarrel like dogs!'

'Yet you come to my table,' the rich man gloats generously.

Yankele is angry, 'I come to you? I come to the fish, the roast, the soup and the sweet vegetables. Are the fish yours more than mine? Did you catch them? Did you raise the ducks? Did you prepare and cook all this? You came to the table which is all set, and I also came here'.

'What would you do if I did not permit you into my home?'

'What does one do with a horse who does not enter into harness? I would collect all the beggars, all the poor, all your servants and leave you standing like a fool in the bathhouse.'

One Sabbath eve his host noticed that Yankele was not dressed as cleanly as usual, so he asked his guest why he was not garbed properly.

'If you the rich would be decent, we the paupers would also be well dressed.'

'This is not true, Yankele. I have given you my suits several times, but you prefer your own poor men's clothing!'

Yankele responded, 'An animal is beautiful in its own skin. The rich are the ugliest animals because they cover their pigskin with the wool of honest sheep. I am ashamed to wear your clothing as if they were mine, and to appear like a wealthy man, which would be a great offence for me.'

Insanity with logic; the host became angry, as if pierced.

Yankele arose, irritated. 'If you want me again at your table you will need to behave more decently, for I have many such fine citizens as yourself.'

He rose angrily and went to another solid citizen, and informed him that henceforth Yankele would be visiting there. The family welcomed him, for his presence brought merriment to the children at the table.

When the hostess asked him jocularly why he did not marry and become like the others, Yankele laughed, 'You won't convince me of such foolishness; to be bound to a Jewish woman and to a household is the utmost in slavery, to which only those who are wise like the rich and labourers can become subject. I will not sell my freedom for eternal labour. A good Sabbath to you.'

Children on the street run after him, pull his jacket, surround him and tease him with their questions. Yankele smiles to each of them, prophesizes their fate. The children laugh and cheer him. They follow and throw pebbles at him all the way to the synagogue where he is safe from them.

Here he opens a volume. The letters dance before him, familiar with the memory of his childhood *kheder* school days. He had read story books. He had been a bridegroom and there was a beautiful girl with long braids.

They had beaten Jews. His father had been killed. She disappeared somewhere. His mother began to sell bagels and he wrote and wrote and always has more to write — even as he speaks, proudly, logically, sarcastically, with a constant humour, addressing himself only to ministers, to rabbis, to scholars, demanding justice for mankind, never for himself. He advises, explains and commands.

Once he wrote to His Majesty advising him to forbid the people to eat dark bread, for there is something in rye to render people insane and leads them to violence. If they will eat white bread they will become normal and wise.

He always signed his letters in Hebrew, 'Jacob named Isaac.'

'How come?', people asked him, 'No one calls you Isaac. They call you only Yankele, or Yankele the Insane'

'Only animals are called by their true names. But authors, scholars have names of their own.'

And Yankele the Insane, without a shirt of his own, no corner of his own, no wife or family, in his fantasy fights the bourgeois, seeks to provide for the world, writes petitions, advises ministers of state, teaches wisdom to mankind and signs with the utmost authority Jacob named Isaac.

So Yankele has been living for years, and everyone in the *shtetl* is satisfied.

Leaving Hamburg
The Dream no More
From the series "To America"
Moshe Samuelson
Keneder Odler, January 5 and 26, 1915

What I wish to narrate began some twenty-four years ago during the stormy period for Jews when the Argentine movement had seized the Jewish people in all its corners like a flame.

The Baron de Hirsch Committee which was located in nearly all major towns in Europe could not cope with this mass migration, and they sent these poor unfortunates wherever they could.

One ship of such wanderers found their way to Montreal, Canada after it spent months between committees, under the impression that they would find land, hoping and dreaming of a Jewish colony, a Jewish settlement and even a Jewish republic.

The leader and the finest of the group was young Abraham Konstaninowsky, an educated Hebraist, from a fine family, age twenty-four, who dreamed the great vision of his people. He left his parents, wife and his children, friends and relatives, to pursue prospects for a happier future, together with comrades.

This grandiose dream burst in Montreal.

For three days the ship of poor immigrants stayed in port. It seemed as if they would be returned, but thanks to the aid of the Baron, they were permitted to land and scatter all over America.

Abraham was sent with his cousin whom he met perchance. (...)

Leaving Hamburg
In that time, Abraham discovered that their hopes of being sent soon to the Argentine were dampened as the movement was temporarily stopped because of an overflow; the rest would be sent somewhere in Canada.

It was a strong blow for Abraham. All day he walked about in a daze. He did not mention it to anyone, not even to Miss Frumer.

But he was soon accustomed to the idea; indeed he saw it as advantageous. It meant that they would move still more Jews from Russia, above the three million to Argentina. In the meantime Jews will also come to Canada. That is, Russia will remain almost without Jews.

He took it for granted that the Jews to be sent to Canada will also be settled on the land, in colonies, with fields, homes, horses, oxen and cows and sheep.(...) A wide open piece of land, once inhabited by the Indians.

(...) 'A million Russian Jews will cultivate the land, build railways, factories and cities, will found a small Jewish republic under English protection; the second republic will be in Argentina.' (...)

He was so excited by this grandiose vision that he barely controlled himself; he searched out Miss Frumer and began to paint the great wonderful picture that his fantasy had created. He held her hands as he spoke with fire, 'Just imagine two Jewish nations, two Jewish republics, with four to five million Jews, in Jewish colonies, with Jewish cities and villages, with Jewish farmers, railways, telegraphs, officials, and not a Jew in Russia, like in Spain, and, like in Spain, they come begging, 'Come back, Jews'.

Miss Frumer stood, her hands in his, believing in none of this, certain that all this is fantasy. But she saw so much beauty in his enthusiasms. Her stubborn eyes suddenly became soft. She barely kept from seizing him to kiss him.

'Beautiful dreamer that your are', she tapped his forehead. 'If I were not a girl I would seriously kiss you. How quickly you build Jewish kingdoms with Jewish republics, colonies and railways' (...)

Abraham looked at her confused gaze. He felt her pulling him down by the hair, far from the high heavens and setting him down on earth...

'You understand. You are...,' he stumbled, 'I cannot believe you. It cannot be (...) It is impossible you love your people. It cannot be otherwise. It is only a question of temperament. Tell me what idea a man represents, and I will tell you his temperament (...) logic, brains are nothing. Logically I can agree with you, on matters that are not connected with, you understand. But I will never agree that my child would be better brought up by a stranger. Regardless of logic, I must be the educator of my child. Whatever education I can give my child, I must give him. This is my temperament saying this, my soul.' (...)

'I understand,' Miss Frumer was smiling. That is why I say you are so beautiful a dreamer' (...)

On the morrow, on Tuesday, registration of immigrants began. There was talk of a ship of immigrants sailing on Saturday. (...)

The Dream No More

'Montreal, Montreal, Canada.'

Suddenly the cry swept the entire ship.

Who was the first to cry this out? No one knows who it was. Possibly there was no first, for the ship suddenly seemed to have turned without notice and all at once everybody saw the shore before their noses.

All was confusion on board. The sailors began to run here and there as if poisoned, with chains resounding, pulling ropes, knocking with hammers and axes.

The first and second class passengers came out, smiling, well dressed, pointing out with their fingers as they lifted up their small children.

The Jews rushed to the deck of the ship, looking about on all sides, straining and confused.

In front of them all stood Abraham and Miss Frumer with papers in their hands, pale and dazed.

At their side was the *shoykhet* with his plush skullcap sticking out from under his cap, with a black silk belt over his Atlas capote with its lining showing, one hand in the belt, the second pulling the thin, blond little beard, trying to see with his short-sighted eyes as if he represented the spiritual leader of these Jewish immigrants.

Near him stood the Siberian with the dark girl and her dimples; with them several youths and young girls, cheerful, wide awake and blushing.

The Siberian imitated each of the *shoykhet*'s gestures, his hand in the peasants belt, and was pulling the mass of his thin beard as the youngsters were choking with laughter

Well dressed men and women appeared on the shore, their faces cheerful and shining. Hands began to wave and handkerchiefs fluttered in the air.

Soon the hands stretched out, eyes winked at eyes and hearts spoke out to hearts.

Two sailors pushed their way to the railing, began to move as if to prepare to work. Slowly, in a minute the ship moved — and then stopped.

Boarding ramps were thrown out from the dock. Men began to push from both ends, closing arms together; chains were ringing, happy outcries, ringing kisses, cheerful love, overjoyed cries. The air was full of joy.

They left the ship, one after another, and they disappeared one after another from the dock, to the last, happy with their beloved ones. Everything was silent and dead. Only cases and boxes from the ship unloading were heard and the rumbling of barrows on the stony port.

The poor Jewish immigrants remained on deck, looking about mutely, with bewildered eyes. No one to say a word to them, to ask them a question, to meet them. (...)

Several hours passed, night was approaching.

The woman and children, heads bowed, sat down again on the deck and the men surrounded Abraham and Miss Frumer, asking 'What will be? Where are they?'

A sea of sorrow, pain and reproach was pressing. Where are the promised treasures? (...)

Abraham and Miss Frumer were ashamed to look them in the eyes. They felt that they had swindled the poor Jews.

Abraham descended from the vessel, seeking to leave the port and come to the city. He saw a street with stone houses, people. He tried to speak to them in Yiddish, German, but no one understood him. He suddenly felt forsaken, alone and defeated. A cry burst from him, 'Master of the universe, for how long yet?[1] When is the limit?'

He returned to the ship to console the poor and beaten Jews. The committee from Baron de Hirsch are delayed, or there is some misunderstanding. As he was speaking to them he came to believe that this is so, that they will come; they must come; it cannot be otherwise!

By night the depressed Jews retired to the dark cabin. An oppressive loneliness spread a sorrow over the entire ship, so that the hearts of the poor Jews swam in blood and tears. They trusted little in Abraham's consoling words and they simply shook their heads as he spoke to them.

In the morning they learned that the ship with all its Jews would be returned because no one had come to receive them.

My pen resigns from the impossible. Human language has no words to recall even a portion of what was happening on this unfortunate ship. Women fainted, bearded men wept like small children; they tore their hair, beat their foreheads with their fists. Surely their cries were heard in the seventh heaven. The planks of the ship soaked in tears and blood. They were ready to jump overboard in desperation.

All day long now men came on board to visit the hopeless, unfortunate wanderers, shook their heads; some of them wrote in their notebooks.

Abraham found a corner of the ship and stared over the railing into the water, as if ossified with confused eyes. Who knows what unfortunate thoughts tangled in his brain. Silent, bereft of language, he sat; his face twisted, his shoulders strained.

Two dark days passed like this. They, poor unfortunates, had wept out their last tears, sighed their final groans, fatigued into indifference to all, to the most earnest and the worst yet to come.

The visitors came oftener, among them some Jews. These spoke to the immigrants and explained that there was no money to help them; they had telegraphed to Baron de Hirsch and everybody was awaiting a reply, in which case something may be undertaken.

The poor Jews had become so much like stone that hope did not move them. They nodded in silence as if to say, 'Enough. We have had enough of such expectations.'

A reply came the third day, the happy day, with money from the Baron. The immigrants were quickly taken into a house not far away.

Their faces shone again. Abraham and Miss Frumer were prepared with their papers. The *shoykhet* stood again, stiff and at arms with his belt and skullcap; the girls again congregated close about the Siberian.

But now it did not take long; they separated in families and as individuals were shipped off to various American regions, in different towns and villages.

'Be Well, Be well.' The breaking up was tearful all about. 'Be well,' Miss Frumer trembled as she bade farewell to Abraham.

'You dreamed a wonderful dream, Konstantinowsky', she told him. 'Now here it is. See here it is'.

She was silent, choked with tears.

'Fare you well, in good health', was all Abraham could mutter. They turned from each other, each wiping tears (...)

---

[1] literally "Until when" *od matai* (Hebrew)

The Little Messiah Infant
Reuben Brainin
Keneder Odler, July 10, 11 and 12, 1912

Caught in another pogrom, they found shelter, together with other Jews hiding out in an attic (...). The infant was crying incessantly, threatening to betray their hiding place. The frightened men and women were afraid, 'We will all die because of him.' I was all the more confused and did not know what to do. I tried rocking him, shaking him, stroking him, feeding him, caressing him, kissing him; but he cried the louder.(...) [The people about me] were the angrier at both of us, as if the baby and I were teasing them. They seemed to hear someone in the attic (...) Our group panicked, the more loudly, crowding each other (...).

Suddenly a pair of hands tore the child from my arms! 'Choke him, suffocate him, the little bastard. Silence him.' But others urgently and quietly cried out 'That Jews should do this! That they should say this like a baited animal!' I lunged for the baby, but he cried the more shrilly as if he was begging with his final powers for his life. He was struggling like a fish in my arms as if to escape me.

'Kill him. (...) We will all be slaughtered because of him. The gangsters heard him. They are coming here. Maybe they are already here.'

A thick hand covered his mouth and choked his cries, nearly suffocating the baby... and through that, redemption was fated not to come. In despair I bit the hand until I could taste the blood. (...) It withdrew.

Suddenly the ultimate tragedy. The door in the floor opened, and a head appeared with stark yellow hair like rigid nails, then a pair of eyes sparking fire, blue fire (...). The hooligan stopped on the ladder, calling down in a hoarse voice, 'Here are the damned Jews, the devils (...). We'll put an end to them, each of them!' (...)

We all froze in silence (...) Only I, seeing my child so endangered, I suddenly felt seized by a mysterious strength. Seeing a heavy scale on the floor, I managed to lift it and hit the gangster over the head. The murderer fell down. In minutes the lower stories were wrapped in terrible flames. In their light which reached us I could see my shining babe. Death was near. Our own noise was tumultuous and I was confused, only one thought tore at my brain: how to save my infant from the flames.

In that minute the Self-Defence came to save us from the fire. Almost as if by magic, they worked quietly, systematically to rescue me and my child and hid us in a basement somewhere. The whole way, like in a nightmare, I saw puddles of drying blood, the limbs of men, broken dishes — a battlefield. In short, we were all rescued, only the old lady in the attic remained; she was not even privileged an Israelite burial.

[But in the cellar I ran into another problem:] My breast had become shrunken, with not a drop of milk, and I could see my child stirring in my arms from hunger (...). I stole out to find a nurse, but in my search a policeman grabbed my infant (...). I begged him on my knees to return the baby.(...) He forced me to kiss his boots and crawl on the ground before him, and he was satisfied and gave me back my baby. But as soon as I began to flee he teased me again, but very angry this time, raising the baby high above his head. (...) I wept for his mercy, but he only kicked me and struck me with his sword so hard that I and the baby fell to the ground (...) He screamed, 'Kill the little devil, or he'll grow up and kill us!' (...)

(...) I picked up my child and fled across the alleyways about (...). I kept hold of the baby and the beneficent angels watched over him — until I fell unconscious. To this day I do not know what happened to me.

(...) I found myself in the basement of the Self-Defence, together with many wounded people. Suddenly I noticed that my baby was not with me! (...) But they told me that he was in safe hands. (...)

(...) If I were to tell you of the sufferings of my baby since it saw the light of day, and then since he was brought to America and then returned to Europe, you would see that this is no ordinary story but a divine intervention and that he will indeed bring redemption. (...)

First Picnic in America
Baruch J. Goldstein
Keneder Odler, November 3 and 4, 1908

This is what my friend began to tell: I had arrived in New York, as you know, the last days of Passover, and so, around *Shavuot* time, a cousin, a girl with thick lips and large grey eyes, told she had ordered a pair of tickets for them for the "picnic" sponsored by the Zhardivke Society (my birth-*shtetl).*

The entire night before the event I tossed about, seeing at first a thick forest with fine chiselled entrance towers, aromatic flowers and grass; those in attendance were finely dressed — a quiet satisfaction on everyone's faces, and I presented myself and entered deep into the forest, hidden by the grown branches like a transparent *succah,* the burning sun, and I, (filled with happy, holy, high good spirits) with my cousin on the soft satin grass, discussing nature. And gradually, as I had long wished, entering into a conversation about "America the Thief," showing her factually that the worthless laws and the vulgar materialism of the life, of she and her friends is — totally opposed to my own.

I can swear that in this dream I smiled naively like a child with the angel of sleep toying with him. (...)

It was my impatience, I think, that awoke me before daybreak and tore me from my bed. I put on my new American blue "suit" with its broad lapels, because I had learned that my cousin was a Yankee and chews a sort of wax and likes men who chew tobacco, and if she is to go out, she says, with a boy, he needs to be a gentleman and must treat her well. With this knowledge I took a few dollars and after rushing through a glass of tea I went to the barber and then to her, to my cousin.

I found her in a state where she would have thrown me out, but for her kind old mother who quieted her down. She was wearing something short and black which showed a red dotted pattern beneath; a loose blouse bound down with pins from the collar; barefoot, unkempt, with her sleeves rolled up as she stood at the washstand, a thick sweat falling down her face to her skirt.

'What a green beast', she called out hoarsely as she saw me 'he's here before dawn' (...)

(...) To make sure I did not observe her in this pose she locked me up in what my cousin called the "bedroom", because it had an iron bedstead with many pillows and coverings for my cousin and her mother to lie on, but also for red American animals. [It] was a dark room. There was a window but it was always drawn with a green "window shade"(...) in the face of a high wall; preserving intolerable dank air.

Alone I stood as on pins in the tiny "bedroom", unable to take a full step. The choice was to stand on one leg or turn in circles.

Only a few hours later, with my dark stone sack opened, my loving smiling cousin met me. (...) I forgave all, even the stench of the bedroom.

[I followed her into the "front room" as she promised me that now she would dress and we would soon be going.]

The minutes were hours as I listened to her mother tell me through her smooth gums for the hundredth time of the teachers and *shokhtim* in her prestigious family, who in all their dreams and nightmares had not seen her in *Ameritskeh*.[1] Heaven knows near what evil man her husband had been buried here in New York, and heaven only knows what will be with her.

By two o'clock my cousin appeared, powdered pale with chalk and red painted lips and a hat with a whole tree of red berries and a pretty sod of grass and flowers; a well pressed skirt that stood independent and crackling, an artificial coquettish smile as she walked straight to the mirror.

'What do you think of my dress?'

'Fine', I answered.

Her mother added, 'Like gold'.

'How do you like my hat?'(ed. note: in English)

'Too many berries, and the grass is too pale.'

But I soon regretted my words. She became still paler. Her eyes almost fell out from her unsheltered eyebrows and sweat appeared on her nose.

'Some expert, this green animal,' she appealed to her mother. '(...)Did you see the flowers on Henny's hat?'

'What does a man know? (...) Your hat is fit for a queen. Wear it in good health. You shine, may no evil eye intervene, like a princess, like a treasure.'

(...)I quickly admitted I was green and knew nothing about American hats.

(...)For endless minutes she pirouetted before the mirror, turned, raised her head and lowered it, pressing at her hips as if her corset hurt her. (...)

[Part 2]

(...)As we left the apartment she courteously gave me her arm.

When we came to the pushcarts she stopped at every vendor and filled every paper bag with apples, plums, herrings, candy, bagels, sausages and mustard and cucumbers and what not. I paid on request, for my cousin told me that it is not polite to bargain when you are out with a lady (...) and the pushcart peddlers know all this. By this time I could not hold her arm. My hands were full and the parcels soggy; I was wet from the juices and from my own perspiration (...) in the midst of the crowding subway passengers who pressed on the bargains in my bags (...)

My cousin found a seat immediately; a sort of a man with a thin nose and racing eyes politely offered her his place as I stood watching her waving her white handkerchief to keep cool, like a true lady.

I know not one word of English, and I still had to buy the "tickets."

(...)Fortunately a Negro with God in his heart decided to descend from the car. I threw my bags on his seat to reserve it.

[Part 3]

By now I regretted the entire excursion: Why the torturous effort and sweating, being pushed by hundreds, blindly stepping on their toes, corns and dresses, for I could not see where I was going with all the parcels in my hands and the tree and grass on her hat and her screeching starched dress and her urging me, (...) 'Faster' (...)

Why the picnic? I nearly spat in my own sweated face(...)

We walked from car to car, often under a merciless sun, eventually on hot sand.(...)

Eventually, both of us fatigued, we climbed a hill, grassy and dust laden.(...)

I threw myself face down; the sun was a little more considerate, even as some berries fell from her hat and as my cousin seized upon the parcels; her teeth working voraciously together with lips and cheeks.

[Part 4]

When the round sun settled on one side my cousin rose with difficulty, shook the crumbs off, looked slowly at her mirror (...) and gave me her arm(...).

At the picnic women with fearsome hats beset with veritable forests, complete birds, eyes, mouths, and several consumptive trees, witnessed children playing in a circle.(...) Wooden two-legged horses on a carousel participated to one side, a heated discussion of young people, shooting high phrases without meaning. Some gentlemen were waiting with their parcels for their ladies on the swings who were frightened and screaming.

Not a sign of the forest or the odour of grass I had dreamed of.

(...)The chants and screaming and the demonic dance of the wild Indians in the desert. (...) 'Let us ride the carousel.'

(...)Out of control, red faced I cried out: 'To hell with your horses!'

---

1. "Ameritskeh" is a pun on "Amerats" from Hebrew "am ha-arets" – ignoramus

Storm Man
Reuben Brainin
Translated into Yiddish by Isaac Yampolsky
Keneder Odler, March 17, 1913

He was and is no more.

It was an alien and remarkable phenomenon.

[What a strange phenomenon he had been, not known to himself or to others: Some considered him crazy, some a genius to be avoided or kept at a distance, feared like a plague. Others loved him, respected him.]

He was a sort of wandering Jew in constant movement, a man of storm, (...) a national anarchist of renaissance, a prophet of the national rebirth.

His beginning is a riddle; his end a tragedy, possibly a comedy.

(He was proud) of his oriental background, from Salonica. Others were convinced he was a Russian. He mastered many languages, European and eastern; his Hebrew was that of a Jerusalemite; his French marked him a Parisian.

In Paris he had studied at the university and was a waiter in a coffee house.

He had warred against the principal men of the whole world and against all governments. He had fallen out with the Quai of Paris, quarrelled with and slapped the face of the chief rabbi of Lyons. He attacked the anti-Semites of Berlin. He fought the anarchists of Switzerland and the anti-Zionists there and the police (...) with whom not?

He mailed threats to the dignitaries of the world, to the president of the United States, to the king of Romania and to Russian ministers, demanding justice from them for his people. (...) He warned Baron de Hirsch that if the magnate will not place his whole fortune at the service of the founding of the Jewish state, he would commit suicide outside his palace. He threatened that he would bomb Dr. Herzl if the founder of Zionism would not adopt the political views of the young men as the Congress program(...) instead of the current milder line. His Zionism was that "Zion must be redeemed with fire and storm and blood, with smoke and fire."[1](...)

(...)I saw him in infinite irritating sorrow in varying phases, in constantly changing phases of the eternal burning nationalist Jew, the flaming Zionist.

(...)[His tales and sermons were a mixture of alternating rays of startling contradictions and alienation.]

He was driven from land to land, from France because of his anarchism, from Vienna on general suspicion, from Berlin because of a sensational scandal, from Switzerland for no given reason.

But, wherever, he was active.

(...)In Belgrade he briefly edited a French-language monthly for Zionism entitled "Carmel"; (...) in Antwerp a daily pro-Palestine newspaper for a month; in Geneva he founded a small society to redeem the Holy Land by the sword; he addressed student groups; he would jump on tables with comments like bombs.

Kant he considered a simple *goy*; Goethe taboo because ugly; (...)Graetz and Geiger were ignoramuses.

He would come to Zionist Congresses with loads of political leaflets and a loaded revolver, in his pocket. But he had to be silent, never called upon to address the convention as a delegate. Once he tried to speak as a Free Zionist, but Herzl dismissed him. He had never stooped for any man, but he recognized the authority of Herzl.

With his soft words and extraordinary loving person Herzl won him over.

He met Herzl in a Basel lane, and began to draw his revolver, but Herzl screamed at him and put his hand on his shoulder; (...)at this he quieted down.

In his heart he entertained a fearful Zionist thought which he seldom intimated to his closest friends. (...) They credited him with strange rumours. But he suddenly cast aside his complex life: at midday on a street in some Italian city. He pulled out his revolver and aimed it at his temple, and fell, not to rise again. A mystery in life and in death.

His name was Marco Boruch.

---

[1] Biblical quote

Question to a Rabbi
Isaac Yampolsky
Keneder Odler, April 6, 1913

Rabbi, I come to ask you whether or not I am bound to perform the thanksgiving prayers. I nearly became a widower today. My woman[1] fell from the attic.

It is three weeks before Passover, but for her it has been *Erev Pesach* ever since Purim. She rests no more than the Sambatyon River and does not sleep nights, and she gives me no rest! I am half sick because of her.

The story of the Passover borsht began right after Purim. So it is natural that the borsht be set? But at first she began cursing me for standing, arms folded and not helping her put the little barrel on four bricks in a corner.

It's her way when something troubles her. She lets it out on my father for having created me.

When the barrel was in place she began to rub off the zinc from its edges and wrapped it about and covered it with a white rag to let the Passover water seep through. By the time I had finished my morning prayers she had done the edges, and had cursed Columbus for inventing America and water zinc. She had cursed the boarder woman upstairs for not coming down to help peel a single beet. During Passover she will come down begging, 'Sheyndl, give me a cup of the borsht!' Nor did I escape scot free. Whenever Columbus and the boarder upstairs come up, I find myself in the middle.

In short, she sits before the sack of beets and peels beet after beet with a Passover blade, holding the beet by the tail and cuts and sculpts it and curses the peasant who had put large beets on top and tiny ones at the bottom. I passed by and kicked a beet which flew to the stove and struck a pot which was not prepared for Passover. She grabbed the beet and threw it at my head. Fortunately it missed me and instead hit the window and broke it and flew outside with the shattered glass. The cat was frightened and ran through the window. I was by this time a bit angry (...), I quoted the verse "the jar broke and we were spared," spit and went out into the street.

When I came home I found the Passover borsht covered with sackcloth, bound with a rope. She was at the table putting black raisins into a large bottle for Passover wine.

'What are you staring at, *golem*?', she said, half in anger. 'Did you never see raisins? Don't put your unclean hands in. Here are some for you. Go choke.'

Generally she is not a bad woman, but still a woman!

She rose early the next morning to prepare the closet to hide the *matzot*. I heard no curses from her that day, for I ran away and did not return until evening.

Her first welcome was, 'What I wished you all day should come to you.'

'Half for you and half for me,' I responded. 'Couples should share equally in joy and in trouble.'

'Woe to your life if ever you run away and leave the entire Passover eve upon my shoulders (...). The Passover wash needs to be prepared. Did you arrange for a woman[2] to help me?'

[I promised to find one for her], but she continued, 'Some man to get me a woman. Just the man to find me a woman. I already have one without your help.'

That morning came the order of the wash; at four it was not possible to come into the house. Beds had not been made for two weeks. The kitchen floor was soaking, with a dark steam like in the bathhouse. The woman was scrubbing with a shovel and she with a pitchfork, her apron folded in the corners, moving from one end of the house to the other. I tell you, rebbe, a spirit was working within her.

Today at dawn she awakened me. 'Yudel, move. He is lying and snoring like in a steam bath.'

'Let me sleep a little,' I pleaded with her. 'I have a headache.'

'A sickness in his bones, a plague in his throat!', she unscrews her sacred mouth on me, early morning fashion. 'It is the eve of Passover. I need to hang the wash in the attic and he wants to sleep like on Sabbath after dinner.'

The baby began to cry, the boys to quarrel. She went down; pinched one, slapped the other; the cries reached heaven.

'He doesn't even care' she screamed at me. I put on my drawers and launched out with the strap as much as I could. She came to their defence.

'Look at him. Haman is inside him.' She seized the children and beat them mercilessly.

[I tried to silence her.] 'Hold your snout,' she answered, 'He got out of the wrong side of the bed. Help me get the wash up into the attic.'

'I am not taking anything to the attic,' I said firmly, and began to get dressed.

'Yudel, today you are getting your black ending from me. Let me see you not taking the wash up for me.'

She climbed up and began to untie the ropes. In the meantime murder left me, and when she called, 'Yudel, *nu!*' I began to lift up the parcels to her one by one. I was standing on the ladder; she was above me, taking each bundle from my hands. When I thought I was finished she called out, 'Why are you standing there? Why are you not climbing to the attic?'

'Why do you need me there?' I called up to her.

'Like a plague I need you (...). Come faster. You will help clean up the mess here. Why are you standing there, my *golem*. It is Passover. Woe to my life!'

In pain and agony I climbed up (...). I began to arrange all the old things that accumulate in a household: an iron hoop, empty bottles, worn out boots, a broken grater. I swept them into a corner. In the pile I recognized my mother-in-law's old *Korban Minchah* ("Sacrifice of the Afternoon"). I turned the pages of the *siddur*, yellow spots at the bottom of the pages from the turning, and I remembered the beautiful old lady with her glasses, reading the Yiddish version on Sabbath afternoons, and reading *thillim* and *tekhines*.

As I had this heritage in my hands in the attic I thought of her and what her thoughts must have been, unknown thoughts.

I tell you, Rebbe, when one sits in high places, one has higher thoughts.

I remember boarding in her home as a greenhorn, meeting my woman who was also green at the time. My father-in-law, peace be on him, was an honest man and something of a scholar. He dealt with chicken and fish, and made a living. He would not let his daughter work in the shop because of the Sabbath. He was sorry for me for having to desecrate the Seventh Day.

When I see her now I remember her then, a beauty and a fine soul. Is she mean now? (...) When we married my father-in-law opened up a grocery store for us on St. Dominique St. and we began earning a decent living. We loved each other. Don't we love each other now?

I remember when my in-laws passed away. He left us a small inheritance. We bought a small property and we manage to live. Our children grow up as Jews. I am a member of both Talmud Torahs. The rabbi receives Succoth *etrog* and Passover gifts. They are talking about electing me president, and I was thinking that others may not agree (...)

Bang! — And my woman fell down from the attic.

I barely dragged her into the bed. She lost a piece of her left ear and twisted her left hand. The doctor says she is in no danger. She will have to stay in bed for two weeks, this before Passover.

I brought you, Rabbi, two ten dollar bills for all institutions. Now, tell me, Rabbi, do I need to perform the *gomel* for her or not?'

[1.] In referring to his wife the narrator uses "*Yideneh,*" or "Jewish woman"

[2.] Here the narrator uses "*goya,*" non-Jewish woman .

A Quebec Story
H. Hershman
Presumed to be in *Keneder Odler,* no date.

Near the banks of the Richelieu River lies the village of St. Simon; its chalky houses and barns reflected in the quiet clear river peering between the trees and sated fields as white splotches on green sheets, dreamy in the afternoon sun.

As if intoxicated by the powerful odour of the sun heated clay fields, the cattle lie tired, their legs behind them in the deep grasses, heedless chewing their cud.

Their (udders) heavy (with) milk, they await with bovine patience, peering into the endlessness for the peasants to come at sunset to drive them to the barns, where they will empty their full contents, when they will again be allowed into the fertile fields.

Several horses stand head to head under the cool shadow of a large maple, widely branched, motionless but for their tails driving their torturing flies. A young pony of undetermined age runs wildly about the high grasses, hastily, then ceases, as if in search, calls hoarsely with his young voice and begins his race far beyond the bushes of young fresh trees.

From the monotonous chicken (yard) and the open garden around a pile of garbage, the fowl scratch with their claws, they find hidden seeds which they collect with their sharp beaks.

Behind the barn a large rooster with a red comb begins to speed toward the camp of hens, but as he approaches them he slows down. With proud steps he turns about a white hen, lets down his wings to the ground, displaying his masculine greatness, and begins to argue with the white hen which listens to nothing, (lifts) her white wings and speeds far and low to another end of the pile.

Angry at the rejected declaration of love, he strides away far more proudly. 'It matters not; you will come begging me yet.' Without even looking about, he returns behind the stall to his own pile of dirt.

From far away the sound of the blacksmith, the hammering of a hammer on an anvil, and the hoarse sound of horses.

All is quiet on the dreamy ways that lead through the village, but sometimes the stillness is interrupted by a passing (load) of hay or the frosty passage of the postman on his way to the railway station at the other end of the village.

Later, when the sun sets in the west and the flaming redness is at last reflected in the golden crest of the church, a damp coolness spreads over the village. Chimneys begin to smoke, the smoke descends over the rivers and over the soft roads with the odour of burning pine wood.

Then the old Abbé Bélanger in his long black *soutane*, circled with his all-coloured belt, appears outside of the church, a small *bréviaire* in hand, on the way to the large store belonging to Samuel Grodsky. When Samuel sees the priest at his store, he bows to him respectfully. Then the two men are seen walking on the only wooden sidewalk leading to the church, deep in an important conversation.

As the peasants drive home from the fields and encounter the priest and the Jew they ask: who is wiser, the priest or the Jew? Though they called him *Le Petit Juif* in the region, the peasants never expressed it with a tone of Jew hatred. For the peasant's tongue could never express his alien name, and because of his limited height, it was always easier to call him the little Jew.

Loaded with two packs of merchandise on his shoulder and on his breast, he had appeared some thirty years ago in the region. Under the heavy burden of the two packs his short body was bent still lower to earth and he knocked respectfully at the doors of the peasant homes with his tablecloths, towels, combs, brushes, needles, thread. Children laughed so much at his erroneous expressions that the elders moralized at them: it is not right to laugh at a stranger. But amongst themselves they whispered: in a few months he will speak correctly, and better than us. No need to worry, we know the Jews;

they are as clever as the devils, these Jews.

The hidden laughter of these people, their considering him from all sides, and his awareness that it was of him that the matter was — all this did not disturb him; nor how they referred to him, as long as they dealt with him; and these villagers did deal with him.

No sooner did he appear at the door of a peasant home, he did not ask whether they needed anything or not, he immediately put down his two large packs and unpacked them on the floor of the house.

The entire family gathered, admiring with smiling friendship the variety of the numerous articles, the colourful merchandise of women's articles, the ingenious inventions which he kept on pulling from his cases, displaying each of them to the eyes of all; see how pretty, how cheap.

Le Petit Juif lost its true meaning in the course of the years, and it appeared as if it were his true name. When after several years he fell in love and married Germaine, the daughter of a wealthy farmer in the area and opened the big store in the village, he clearly wrote (it) in golden letters, and all knew that *Le Petit Juif* was the owner of the place, and came to him from the surrounding villages for many years as his customers. The nature of his trade was great and he devoted himself to his business entirely. He left the education of his children to Germaine for years and almost forgot his origin.

Jacques' education was that of all French Canadian children, purely in the pure Catholic spirit. Were it not for his friends who constantly reminded him that his father was a *Juif*, and that he himself had a share in Jesus' murder, it would never have come to his mind to think of his birth. He had thought of it only as a child, and when he grew into a strong lad and (was) in quarrels with his pals, and they threw his birth up to him again, with the usual accusations, they soon learned from him that it was not worthwhile to make this kind of trouble with him, and they continued respecting him. But it did leave an impression upon him and feelings awoke in him which were quite alien hitherto.

Now, when he would come into the city on his father's business, and he would meet Jewish merchants, he would also show an interest in matters that had no connection with his business and would begin to feel comfortable in the Jewish environment. When he came to know Esther, the bookkeeper in one of the wholesale houses in the large city nearby, it never occurred to him that they were not equals, and that there was an abyss between them.

With the charm of a handsome wealthy youth whom the village girls would never reject, he attempted to become closer from his first meeting with her, but she coyly was distant.

Jacques was a frequent visitor in the city, particularly in the store where Esther was bookkeeper. His too frequent visits to the office drew attention, she told him once. She could not see why he was spending so much time in the city even while he was certainly needed at home at a time when his business here was at an end; to which he told her that of his major business he had not yet begun to speak.

His excessively frequent stays in the office were also noticed by the other employees and they began to exchange sharp comments at his and her expense: 'The *shaygetz* has precious eyes,' and 'No need to pull at his tongue'. The old bookkeeper sitting at his high stool, gray head buried in the thick volumes, was speaking to himself. 'No one who is uncircumcized will refuse Yiddish (...) in Jewish girls; the entire universe is one.' And the long bachelor with spiky complexion looked at her jealously as he added, 'There is no difference between his six-pointed cross which he wore and a four-pointed cross; it is all an idol.'

Esther avoided speaking much about this but she did suffer, of the thoughts that had been long torturing her. She knew that he was not indifferent to her and that the longer she knew him, the closer he became to her. It was a difficult test.

Many were the nights she did not sleep looking for a justification for the plans she was contemplating — and in vain.

That morning she left the house earlier than usual, and the others also wondered. So early? The church bell had not yet rung! Esther was silent.

Only when she came out she remarked how early it was, how the street was different, cleaner and more free. During the day it was so narrow here. Even the thoughts did not have so much space, and now she could think freely. Would she reach a conclusion, a declaration?

Now the ordinarily noisy streets were quiet. The dumb clapping of the horses' shoes on the not quite hardened asphalt could be heard, and soon a baker's wagon came to a standstill at the end of the road, a fatigued young lad descended and thoughtlessly rang the bell of a house next door. A sleepy woman responded from an upstairs window, 'Nothing today'. A sleepy storekeeper opened the door of his store dragging out empty orange crates on which he soon displayed his various greens. He looked about and emitted a clumsy yawn which resounded from the walls in the morning stillness.

It was too early for the office so she made her way through side streets. She would arrive in due time. Sunk in her thoughts, undirected and wandering in the streets, she soon approached her office and noticed only now by the clock on the church tower that she was very late. The tall stipple-faced bachelor was standing on a double ladder at a wall of paper cartons and putting them in order. Hearing her come in he said to himself, 'He has been here quite early. The *goy* is quite obsessed. Probably spent the night with her.' She was not even listening to him. With a double entendre and mischievous smile, 'Possibly this is not new to her. Her coming late now has a connection.'

She was not listening to this either. She had long dismissed him.

Later, when Jacques came into the office, she met him intentionally with an extraordinary warmth; She needs to see him urgently, but she is busy now; could he come in late in the day. She needs to speak to him.

She could not understand exactly what she had told him, but she knew that she had much to discuss, yet she had just decided that morning that she would not. But now the hidden desire emerged so suddenly. How had it happened? But she was happy now that without preparations the beginning was made, a beginning which would lead to an end to much of her thinking without any declaration. (She was) impatient as she had not been until this hour for that which she had awaited, until when she closed the office.

They met in the evening, when the streets were full of people returning home from their daily occupations. Now the sidewalks were narrow for the homebound, roughly jostling each other.

Tenderly he took her arm and helped her through the crowd. She shivered lightly at his first close touch, at the shock through her body, at the strange warmth that reached her heart. Would they not be better on a side street? Yes, he also thought so.

The rich and quiet side streets where they were now walking seemed as dead. The homes were distant from each other, separated from each other by fruit trees and flower beds, now deserted, the residents at their summer homes, doors and windows boarded up; only rarely a remaining servant trimming the trees with long shears.

The knocking of the shears over the dry branches resounded in the evening silence mixed with sounds of a belated woodpecker. From the distance (came) the ringing of the city's tramways, the whistling of locomotives and of the ships which come or go from the port.

Walking quietly and still silently on the quiet streets Esther began to be afraid of herself. The nearness of this powerful fine young man who was not indifferent to her cast a pleasant fear lest she let herself go. She did not even look at his side, but walked at the edge of the paved sidewalk with her summer parasol. Her heart beat stronger, and her mind was mingled with many thoughts, not knowing where to begin; she regretted coming here. In consequence he told her that in fact he knew what it was she wanted to discuss with him; he understood that it was her modesty that prevented her; he would therefore attempt to clarify the situation and seek a response to her unformulated queries.

She listened to his words which were composed of the full truth and naive peasanthood; even though she saw all he did she could not decide to determine all on the spot, and could not promise to accept his invitation to spend a fortnight of vacation in their village.

It was harvest time when Esther openly came to the village. The first several days were virtually a renewal of the soul. It was long since she was so close to raw earth. Once she bent down to knead a piece of black earth between her fingers. A refreshing spirit swept her when she sensed its odour.

She walked hours alone on the loamy road at the side of the rich grain and fields, watching the peasants cut the golden wreaths, binding them in rows until the wagon would take them into barns where the grains would be processed.

From the fields came the songs of the reapers with the sound of the sharpeners over the steel instruments and the life of the insects strolling about the fields and, experiencing again the memories of near-forgotten years of childhood, she barely remembered how she came here and the great change which might possibly come over her life soon.

Only in the evening, as she approached the house where Jacques' father and the old priest were: 'Jacques' bride,' the father told the priest. Looking over his glasses the priest nearly said to himself 'Like the Holy Virgin'.

Since her arrival in the village Jacques avoided discussing his plans with her about his future, waiting for a suitable moment when she would be alone and able to consider all better.

But his father spent much time with her, talked much and proved to win her on their side, covering her with paternal love as if she were already one of his own.

But the mother and the others of the household dealt with her with careful coolness. The whole matter was not near to their hearts. When the family began to prepare for the great annual procession of each fall harvest, the mother asked,

'Will she participate in the procession?'

'No.'

'What will she do that day?'

'She will see how everybody is rejoicing.'

'And she will do nothing?'

'It is not her festival.'

'And she will not go to church to hear the fine prayers and songs?'

'No.'

The mother walked out of the room with a hidden anger.

Since early morning all roads in the area were full of migrants with participants in the procession.

To avoid the thick dust rising from the dry loamy roads many had come before dawn, dressed in their holiday clothing in which they were very uncomfortable.

The great courtyard of the church was full of hundreds of wagons of all styles: light buggies with dreary rubber wheels, shining black against the sun; heavy wagons loaded with hay and light two-wheeled sulkies, with trained ponies for racing.

Horses roamed about unsaddled, their (drivers) chatted about the saddles and of the coming harvests and crop, and the hay prices expected the coming winter, or races about to be held soon in the village, about the entries expected to participate, and foretold the winners and the odds.

Women and the elderly were in the church where Abbé Belanger was preaching, praising the Lord for the crop and awakening pious thoughts.

She found herself restless this morning, out of sorts with herself, looking for a spot where she could be alone. All the rooms were noisy with much coming, going and loud talking, laughing and exchanging country jokes. Guests and Jacques' mother's family came from the countryside. Seeing Esther, they whispered, 'Jacques' bride.' Young girls remained (behind), their foolish hands, embarrassed, unable to speak to her as they looked at her, which only embarrassed her more, unable to free herself; out of doors she would draw more attention. She was glad at the news that the procession would soon begin and that all who would participate must gather at the gathering spot.

As Jacques was leaving the house he came into her room and attempted to explain his leaving her alone. Certainly he would wish to have her accompany them, but he did not wish to convince her. He would soon come back. She was thinking of something else and not even hearing his words. She only nodded, 'Go, go.'

Only when all the close people went out to the great square and lined up for the procession before the church she felt how strange all this about her was, and how deep was the abyss that separated her from these people.

No doubt Jacques loved her, and she him. But they were from two distinct worlds which will never level. Their feelings and conceptions were alien and different and they could never become close friends.

Suddenly she heard the strong pealing of all the church bells, the heavy great basso bells, monotone, sad, with seconds between them, assisted by smaller bells with cheerful melodies which bring a sort of harmony and cast a cheerful sadness upon listeners.The procession had begun. Unwillingly she approached the window and stood behind the curtain whence she could see all. Two quite young priests in long red robes, with white shirts and embroidered edges over their shoulders reaching to the belt. They walked at the end holding little chains with brass vessels filled with smoking aromas swinging side to side, singing Latin hymns, always concluding with the repeated *Kyrie Eleison*.

Facing them, under a silken golden-sketched canopy borne by four old men, was the old priest Bélanger in his priestly garments, white head uncovered, quietly mumbling a prayer.

On both sides two other young priests with dark caps on their heads; as they heard the light sound of a small bell they raised their bass voices to sing a sort of prayer in Latin to which a group of children behind them responded *Amen.*

At some distance from these groups came the flag bearers who carried flags with various pictures of the New Testament, of the crucifixion, of the setting star of Bethlehem. A terrible, unaesthetic picture of blood-covered Jesus, his hands and feet attached by nails to a wooden crucifix, his forehead circled by sticking thorns.

Then came the women led by an elderly matron who could barely lift her feet and was therefore supported by two nuns in long grey. Among them Esther saw Jacques' mother, head bent, with a black chain of many beads, muttering a prayer.

Finally came the youths of Jacques' community dressed in their holiday black. Jacques was carrying in his right hand a large white lit candle bound in white silk, and a small book in his left hand. Seriously he sang hymns with the group. They were supported by two rows of very young children marching at the side in white skirts over their costumes.

(Then came) the column of the very young boys supported by the girls of the society, but Esther could not follow it. Seeing Jacques in this role, she shuddered and drew the curtain with shuddering hand and went back to her room.

Now she began to understand the meaning of the sacred images which decorated her room, the picture of the sacred mother with the tiny child in her arms, beneath the oil-filled lamp which spread a cloister aroma over the room. She looked at the painting which seemed so innocent, (but) had for generations been the motif of endless massacres of millions of Jewish women,

men, and of children.

Under the influence of the procession her thoughts permitted the images of events which she had never experienced, but of which she had read and read, of the letters which her relatives received from their *shtetlekh*, of such processions which had ended in more than blood baths. Before her eyes stood vivid all her massacred kin and it seemed to her now that here went all her kin in skeletal form, frigid, in groups in the very house, one with a hand missing, another a foot, limbs chopped by the murderers. In the deep sockets, a distant emptiness which can see nothing, only a dampened far voice as from a grave where the teeth bit at clasped hands, with wrists pointing to her as they groaned, 'You would join our murderers. A flood of woe upon you.'

A shudder of cold sweat poured over her and soon a frightening heat; the sweat turned into seething water. She opened the window and could see the procession had already proceeded far from the house. She could still hear the strong sound of the peal of the church bells and the distant song of the procession.

The experience of the day had provoked her fear and she was certain that she would not survive the day. She would die, during their day. They would convert her after she had died, and (she would) be buried here in the Catholic cemetery. She must leave.

Late at night when all about her had taken on a dead silence, and all the efforts of the day had been subsumed in a joyous sleep, she left the house with quiet steps. With feverish haste she ran along the river, along the loamy path to the long bridge, far to where the river narrows and begins to roar over the stones and becomes a mighty waterfall.

Some frogs who had fallen asleep were awakened by her arrival and, frightened, jumped into the grasses.

The faster and further she ran, afraid to look back, it seemed that she was fleeing a pogrom, and not alone but with an army of Jews, men, women and children with her, and behind them more wild killers screaming 'catch them; catch the Jews, they crucified our God!' — and she heard the song of last night's procession, *Kyrie Eleison*.

Glossary

batlan / batlanim: an impractical, idle person
batlones / batlanut: impracticality
beys din: rabbinical court
beys hamidrash: prayer house
bikur kholim: society for visiting the sick
biluim: Jewish students' movement started in Russia in the 1880s, dedicated to
    creating agricultural settlements in Palestine
bréviare: Catholic prayer book
Bund: Jewish Socialist political party founded in Russia in 1897
Eretz Israel: Land of Israel
Erev Pesakh: the evening preceding Passover
Erev yom tov: the evening preceding a religious holiday
Erev Yom Kippur: the eve of the Day of Atonement
etrog: a fruit resembling a lemon used for the celebration of Sukkot
fargoyshert: an assimilated Jew
Folksbibliotek: The Montreal Jewish Public Library
Forvertz: Socialist newspaper founded in New York in 1897
gabay: person responsible for the administration of a synagogue
galut: diaspora
gan-eden: Garden of Eden or by extension a place worthy of note
gaon / geonim (pl.): man of great intellectual ability
gmiles khesed / gmiles khsodim: free loan society
golem: a malevolent ghost spirit
gomel: thanksgiving prayer for escaping a grave danger
goy / goyim (pl.): a male gentile
griner / griners (pl.): a recent immigrant
guberniye: a province in Czarist Russia
haggadah: book of prayers used for the *seder* during Passover
hakhnoses-orkhim : Sabbath shelter for the needy
halbdeutsch: a half assimilated East European Jew
Hanuka: Festival of lights
jargon: a derogative term for Yiddish
kashrut: Jewish dietary laws
kav ha yosher, reshit khokhma: studies on the meaning of life, general philosophy
kehillah: network of Jewish community institutions as often found in
    East European towns
kheder: traditional school for young children
kherem: a banishment of the community on a religious basis
khusid: the follower of a Hassidic *rebbe*

kultur: culture

landslayt: a compatriot in the sense of a person born in the same
  locality in Eastern Europe

landsmanshaft / landsmanshaftn (pl.): an association of *landsman*, or persons
  originating from the same town in the Old World

latkes: potato pancakes

loshn kodesh: Hebrew; literally, the "holy tongue."

malbush arumim: society whose goal is providing clothes to the poor

mame-loshn: the Yiddish language as used by native speakers

maskil / maskilim: proponent of the Jewish Enlightenment

matza / matzot: unleavened bread made especially for Passover

menorah: a seven-branched candelabra

minyan / minyonim: a quorum of ten men required for praying

parnas : the president of a synagogue

rebbe: the head of a community of *Hassidim*

roman / romanen (pl.): a novel

samovar : Russian tea kettle

seder: meal performed as a religious ceremony on the first two evenings of *Pesakh*

shames / shamosim (pl.): caretaker of a synagogue

shaygets: gentile male

shekhita: system of ritual slaughtering according to Jewish law

shema: a daily prayer recited by Jews

shirah: religious song of praise

shoykhet / shokhtim (pl.): a ritual slaughterer

shtetl / shtetlekh: a small town in Eastern Europe during the time of the great
  migration, where the majority of the population is Jewish

shul: synagogue

siddur: prayer book

simkha: joy and by extension a celebration

soutane: cassock

succah: shelter built at the time of Sukkot to commemorate time spent in the
  desert by Jews fleeing Egypt

Tageblat: Yiddish Zionist daily founded in New York in 1885

tekhines: prayer book for women

Thillim: the Psalms

tohu bohu: chaos (Hebrew, as used in the first chapter of Genesis)

treyf: forbidden food according to Mosaic law

tsadik: a saintly man

Tsukunft: socialist Yiddish monthly published in 1892 in New York

Yahoudim: members of the early Montreal Jewish families

yeshiva / yeshivot (pl.): a religious academy of higher learning

Dossier Québec Titles from Véhicule Press

Renewing our Days: Montreal Jews in the Twentieth Century
Edited by Ira Robinson and Mervin Butovsky

Putting Down Roots: Montreal's Immigrant Writers
Elaine Kalman Naves

Montreal of Yesterday: Jewish Life in Montreal, 1900-1920
Israel Medres
Translated from the Yiddish by Vivian Felsen

Painting Friends: The Beaver Hall Women Painters
Barbara Meadowcroft

Other Titles of Interest

When Paupers Dance
Szloma Renglich
A novel translated from the Yiddish by Zigmund Jampel

In the Heart of Warsaw
Szloma Renglich
A novel translated from the Yiddish by Zigmund Jampel

Open Your Hearts: The Story of the Jewish War Orphans in Canada
Fraidie Martz

I Am First a Human Being:
The Prison Letters of Krystyna Wituska
Edited and translated by Irene Tomaszewski

So Others Will Remember: Holocaust History and Survivor Testimony
Edited by Ronald Headland

A Rich Garland: Poems for A.M. Klein
Edited by Seymour Mayne and B. Glen Rotchin

Véhicule Press
www.vehiculepress.com